THE **mananam** SERIES

D1496899

Education
Toward Inner
Transformation

CHINMAYA PUBLICATIONS
CHINMAYA MISSION WEST PUBLICATIONS DIVISION

CHINMAYA PUBLICATIONS
CHINMAYA MISSION WEST PUBLICATIONS DIVISION

Chinmaya Publications
Chinmaya Mission West Publications Division

P.O. Box 129
Piercy, CA 95587, USA

Distribution Office
560 Bridgetowne Pike
Langhorne, PA 19053
Phone: (215) 396-0390   Fax: (215) 396-9710
Toll Free: 1-888-CMW-READ (1-888-269-7323)
Internet: www.mananam.org
www.chinmayapublications.org

Central Chinmaya Mission Trust
Sandeepany Sadhanalaya
Saki Vihar Road
Mumbai, India 400 072

Credits:
Editorial Advisor: *Swami Tejomayananda*
Consulting Editor: *Swami Shantananda*
Series Editors: *Neena Dev, Margaret Dukes, Rashmi Mehrotra*
Editorial Assistants: *Rupa Junnarkar, Vinni Soni*
Cover Graphics: *Neena Dev, David Dukes*
Inside Photos: *Eric Ferguson*
Production Manager: *Arun Mehrotra*

Library of Congress Control Number: 2006926987
ISBN: 978-1-880687-60-4   1-880687-60-7

Contents

Part Three

TEACHERS AND SCHOOLS

Part Four

THE STUDENTS

Preface

When we hear the word "education," immediately a vision of schools, papers, computers, and teachers comes to mind. Math equations, chemical reactions, and English assignments tend to haunt us! But is this what education truly is? If this "education" guaranteed a full life, a peaceful life, a way to help with life's ups and downs, then it would be great! But it does not. We all know many "highly educated" individuals whose lives are a mess, and high-profile individuals, such as world leaders and other professionals, who have committed horrendous acts. "Information learning" does not prepare us completely for life's journey and the peace and happiness for which we yearn.

True education goes beyond training to earn a living. It is a lifelong process, which encompasses the art of living; understanding the values of life and infusing them in our day-to-day lives at school, at work, and at home. Learning opportunities are abundant within all our experiences and through all the teachers around us. This is the topic of *Education: Toward Inner Transformation*.

The authors in Part One, show how true education should be a lifelong journey toward self-knowledge and wholeness, rather than simply a gathering of facts, figures, and skills. The sages and saints, and many educators have given us this vision over the centuries. They focused on educating the whole person which would lead toward the ultimate goal of life; lasting peace and happiness. In Part Two, the authors talk about the important role parents play as teachers in their children's lives, beginning even before a child is conceived. The authors in Part Three discuss the role of the teacher. The voices of today's educators and of the past agree that an ideal education should include nurturing the child's spirit. They also write that the teachers have to inculcate and model the values that they want their students to learn. The final essays in Part Four recommend ideas and ideals for students to live by so that an inner transformation can take place. They can then render a great service, not only to themselves, but to the entire world.

A fully educated person lives a dynamic, wholesome, and contented life. This is the vision of education presented by the authors in this book.

The Editors

PART ONE

True Education

*Education is not a filling in of something from outside.
It is a drawing out from within of the highest
and best qualities inherent in the individual.
It is the cultivation and development of these worthy
talents and qualities in an intelligent and rational
way, so as to help build a balanced personality.*

Swami Sivananda

All over the world we find that educational institutions give importance to reading and writing, to new learning techniques, and to better buildings and equipment. Generally there is progress in all those areas which make us smart, but education of proper values and vision of life is lacking. When these same brilliant young people, so successful in academia, get caught in the emotional problems of life, they lose all their efficiency and their objectivity becomes zero. So what is it that educational institutions should pay attention to? The first point is to recognize that the purpose of education is to learn. Then comes the application of that learning, meaning that whatever we have learned we should know how to use it.

Finally, and most importantly is the ethical consideration. We should know the purpose for which our knowledge is to be used. Thus, the aim of education must be examined carefully. We need to ask ourselves, "What is our final objective?" The Sanskrit word *upādhi* means "that which brings about change." That is why in India a university degree is called *upādhi*. After a child has gone through twelve or more years of schooling we expect to see a change in knowledge, behavior, and conduct, an inner transformation, and not just an outer or superficial change.

Swami Tejomayananda

I

What Is True Education?

by Swami Jyotirmayananda

Education is meant to bring out your hidden talents, and to enable you to discover your essential nature and fulfill the purpose of your existence. In so doing you serve humanity in the best way possible. For the vast majority of people, however, the concept of education is extremely limited. People who have big titles or degrees from universities are recognized as educated people and, relatively speaking, that definition is perfectly correct. However, from the point of view of the ideological and philosophical understanding of education, that definition remains shallow. To simply have big degrees and a lot of recognition and titles does not imply that the person is educated in the true sense.

To be educated, in the more profound sense, implies to be able to develop your human potential and higher human values, to be able to handle your mental stress, to be able to live with people with adaptability, and to develop the divine qualities of the soul: humility, goodness of the heart, compassion, selflessness. If these are lacking, one is not educated.

Let me relate to you a well-known parable: Once a group of scholars entered a boat; one was a mathematician, another was a literary giant, another was a scientist. In the course of conversation, each asked questions of the boatman. The mathematician asked him, "Have you ever read a treatise on mathematics, or have you had any experience with mathematics?" And the boatman said, "No. Just counting some mangoes and vegetables, but nothing beyond that." The mathematician replied, "Then you have lost half of your life since you have never had the joy and the thrill one experiences by possessing mathematical talent." The boatman felt miserable, and said, "What can I do? I was born in a poor family; I could never be educated."

Similarly, the scientist spoke about the wonderful strides taken in physics, in chemistry, in astronomy and so many other branches of science. "Do you have any idea," he asked the boatman, "about the vastness of knowledge in science?" And the boatman said, "No. I am just a poor man." "Then you have lost half of your life by missing so much joy."

And the literary man said, "Have you read Shakespeare or any other great poet? Have you experienced the joy of reading novels?" The boatman replied, "No, I have read nothing. I am illiterate." Now they all pitied him, and he himself felt very miserable.

But as the boat proceeded on its course through the river, it was caught by a whirlpool that tossed it from side to side. At this point the boatman said, "Do any of you know how to swim? Now we are in a difficult predicament and we may have to jump." And they all replied, "No, we do not know how to swim!" The boatman said, "Well, if that is the case, now all of your lives are gone!"

The moral of this story is that you may have great talents, you may be a computer expert, you may be a great mathematician, you may know how to erect a bridge or build a condominium, but when certain problems develop at home, can you handle them? When you suddenly hear something shocking — the doctor informs you that you have a terminal disease — what happens to your mental balance?

When some challenging situation actually develops in life, all your accomplishments do not come to your aid; then you feel as if you are drowning. On the other hand, there are people who are not so educated from the academic point of view, but they can handle stressing situations, they keep calm in adversity, they have a mature judgment in difficult situations, they can advise others, they radiate a sense of comfort and inspiration for others. Are not these people more educated than so many students that are being manufactured by so many universities year after year?

The educational system, as it was in Vedic times, was geared to enable a student to serve himself and society. Therefore, it was founded on discipline. Anyone who entered the school had to follow the path of *brahmacarya*, which meant a complete discipline of the body, mind, and senses.

In those times, every form of learning was called a *veda*. If you were interested in martial arts you studied *Dhanur-Veda*, and you learned archery under a guru who taught you *mantra* (secret formulas) related to archery. First, he disciplined you well and then, when he found you qualified, he taught you archery. If you were interested in medicine, you had to follow the disciplines of *Āyur-Veda*. Every branch of knowledge was considered a *veda*, which implied that whatever you were learning you learned with humility and with a spirit of serving God in humanity, always keeping in view the goal of life — Self-realization.

The Four Purposes of Life

In order to understand education in its integral way, you should understand the four purposes of life: *dharma, artha, kāma,* and *mokṣa. Dharma,* or the cultivation of ethical values, is the basic purpose of life and the foundation of education. All that you achieve and learn should be based on *dharma,* or righteousness. You must possess a clear and sublime conscience. If *dharma* is not there, all your learning is in vain.

If *dharma* is not there, all learning and accomplishment bring about a demoniac development. A person who is undisciplined and unethical may suddenly tumble upon an important discovery, and be considered a great man in the eyes of others. However, from a philosophical and spiritual point of view, if his discovery is intended to become a source of misery for others, then that is a demoniac achievement.

Therefore, education must have its roots in *dharma.* The guiding line in an ideal educational system must be to promote harmony and goodness in people. One should never step beyond the principles of nonviolence, truth, and purity. Greed, violence, and passion must not be given license, but are to be controlled. If a student starts his studies as a doctor, for example, with his mind set upon the idea that "one day I am going to be a millionaire and drive a Rolls Royce," then he is off to a poor start in the light of dharma. Although he may set up a wonderful dispensary or hospital, if money is his main inspiration, then his medical attainment is not the product of true education. Although that is the type of education that the majority of people are seeking now, it is not real education.

People crave for pleasure, and pleasure seems to be the goal of the present educational process. Students dream of having lots of money and power — the wealth to go anywhere they want and the resources to own anything they want. However, an education that caters mostly to these values is not education, and an intellect that schemes for these things is called *bhoga buddhi*, an intellect that wants only enjoyment.

There is an ancient saying from the *Mahābhārata: Sukhārthinaḥ kuto vidyā* — "There is no knowledge for one who loves comfort." If you are a lover of pleasure and comfort, there is no knowledge for you. You are not qualified for education. *Kuto vidyārthinaḥ sukham* — "If you are a student, how can there be comfort?" There is no comfort for you if you truly seek knowledge. To shun comfort and luxury is not a miserable development, but rather a joyous development.

Imagine a student who is just twenty-five years old and wants his head propped up by a soft pillow on an easy chair; he doesn't want to do anything but move little buttons on a computer and expects his parents to do all the heavy jobs at home. Outsiders observing the student may think he has become well-educated, but what type of person will he become later? Life presents so many threatening and challenging situations; if one has not been disciplined, if one is not accustomed to hard work, he is ill-prepared to face these challenges.

While teaching children one must not be overprotective and thus spoil the child. If a child is not accustomed to having his ego shaken a little, if he has not developed any patience and endurance in bearing insult and injury, he has not been cultivating *dharma* as the foundation of his education.

The second purpose of life is *artha,* or economic position. Money is a means to a higher end. Just having money does not mean anything at all. Observe how so many people gain millions of dollars overnight in the lottery, yet that doesn't make any difference in the deeper quality of their lives. All the defects in their personalities can even become more exaggerated! This effect is similar to what happens when you look into a magnifying mirror: when there was no magnification, your face looked gentle and fine; but look into a strong magnifying glass and you become a giant and every hair looks like a big pole! That is what suddenly becoming rich can do — it does not in any way make you a better person.

On the other hand, if you are earning money with a basic grounding in *dharma,* then the money that comes to you becomes a means to your self-improvement, a means to helping society by performing good deeds. Used in this manner, it will not stir your vanity.

The next and third purpose of life is *kāma,* or developing social relationships. That is also a part of education. If you cannot adapt and adjust to your friends and live in harmony with family members, then life becomes empty.

No matter where you are or in what situation you are placed, you always find the challenge of different relationships. If you cannot handle people with different moods and egocentricities, then life becomes empty.

A person cannot live alone. Even if you were in the Himalayas, you would find that you were making friends with monkeys, birds or squirrels. You would find some relationship to overcome loneliness.

Kāma is the vital value of life that allows you to live in harmony with others so that you are then free to plan how to help all humanity. To be able to expand and outgrow one's ego is the most profound aspect of education. A truly educated person is inspired by compassion to help others, and he places every talent he has in the service of others. In that way his talents increase more and more. Selflessness is the secret of discovering more and more talent and abundance within.

Mokṣha, or Liberation, is the ultimate purpose in life. The entire educational process should lead you to Liberation. In this stage the knowledge that you gain is known as *parā vidyā.* The *Upanishad* say there are two types of *vidyā,* or knowledge: *aparā* and *parā.*

Aparā is the lower knowledge or relative knowledge, the knowledge that helps you in your daily life. Within that category of knowledge comes all the sciences and the arts, all the subjects that are taught in universities. *Parā vidyā,* however, is the knowledge that is mystical. When you practice concentration and meditation and are guided by a guru, then you discover a knowledge that brings about a complete fulfillment of the urge to know. *Parā vidyā* is that knowledge by which all is known.

Parā vidyā is the attainment in which all educational systems must culminate. That is the goal. Keeping this in view, an ideal student should develop self-discipline; he should strive to develop virtuous qualities like humility, patience, sincerity, and simplicity; he should practice self-introspection and austerity; he should be self-dependent; he should flow out of himself in service to humanity and thereby commune with God. These are the great highlights of true education. If you have these, you are really educated. Anything other than this is a deviation — lack of education. May God bless you with the purity of intellect that leads you to health, long life, peace, prosperity, success, and Liberation!

II

Questioning the Aims of Education

by Nel Noddings

I want to turn now to an examination of practices that should raise questions about the aims of education. It is often helpful to see a familiar scene through the eyes of an intelligent and sympathetic stranger,[1] so let's pretend that a visitor from another world has visited our schools and wants to share his or her observations with us. The visitor talks with a representative educator (Ed).

Visitor: It struck me as odd that, although your people spend much of their time in homemaking, parenting, and recreation, these topics are rarely addressed in your schools.

Ed: That's because we regard the school as a somewhat specialized institution. Its job is to teach academic — the material that cannot easily be taught at home. Homemaking, parenting, and worthwhile forms of recreation are taught at home. Indeed, most of us believe that it would be an improper intrusion into family life for schools to teach such topics.

Visitor: Ah, yes. This is part of your liberal heritage, is it not? But what is done about the children who come from homes where these matters are not taught well? From what I've seen, there are many such children.

Ed: You're right, and this does worry us. However, we believe that people who have a thorough command of the fundamental processes will be able to learn these other matters on their own. They will have the skills to do so. And they will qualify for good jobs, so they will be able to provide the material resources characteristic of good homes.

Visitor: Hmm. Well, of course, there is something to that. But if children from poor homes (not necessarily poor in the financial sense, you understand) have great difficulty learning, it would seem that a society ought to attack the problem at all levels — do something to eliminate poverty, encourage adult interest in homemaking and parenting, and teach these things in school.

Ed: But parents don't want us to do this! They don't want the schools to prescribe methods of parenting or to pronounce one way of homemaking better than another. We have a hard time teaching any sort of values in our schools.

Visitor: You would not want to indoctrinate, I understand. But these topics need not be presented dogmatically. In your English classes, high school students could read and discuss children's literature. In social studies, they could study the development of the home and forms of housing. In art, they might study the aesthetics of homemaking. In science, child development. In foreign language, patterns of hospitality might be studied. In mathematics, they might look at statistical studies that show the high correlation between socioeconomic status and school achievement. These are just examples, of course.

Ed: And very good examples! However, our schedules are already so full that I don't see how we could make room for all these things.

Visitor: Perhaps, if you will forgive my saying so, you haven't thought deeply enough about what you are trying to do.

Ed: We want to give all children the opportunity to learn what they need to succeed in our society. All children!

Visitor: That is commendable, very fine. But how do you define success? Have the schools failed a child if he wants to become an auto mechanic? Do they help a girl who wants to be a beautician?

Ed: We believe they should make those choices later. First, get a sound, basic education.

Visitor: In watching many classes and talking to many students, it seems that — because their interests and talents are ignored in school — many young people fall into these occupations instead of choosing them proudly. They feel they are not good enough for more desirable work. There is an injury inflicted on them.

Ed: We are getting off the subject. What has this to do with teaching homemaking and the like?

Visitor: It has to do with happiness, and that was my reason for bringing up those topics in the first place. If happiness is found in domains other than salaried work, shouldn't those other domains be treated in education? And since one's occupation also influences happiness, that too should be included in education. But I was just getting started. ...

Ed: I hesitate to ask.

Visitor: It seems that your society, your government anyway, has been waging a losing war on drugs, —

Ed: Now I've got you! We *do* teach about the dangers of drug abuse.

Visitor: Yes, yes. But your television commercials are filled with ads for drugs, some of them quite dangerous. Do you help students to see how they are being manipulated?

Ed: Well, we worry most about illegal drugs.

Visitor: Have you noticed that many teenagers from low socio-economic status neighborhoods wear expensive name-brand clothing? They could clothe themselves for far less money and perhaps avoid taking part-time jobs that keep them from their studies.

Ed: So you want us to engage in consumer education as well as homemaking, parenting, and — you're not finished, are you?

Visitor: Perhaps we should let it be for now. It just seems so sad that, when everyone seeks happiness, the schools do so little to promote it.

Ed: Well, I promise to think more about it. (Shaking his head) I just don't see what we can do.

FOOTNOTE:

[1] This is a familiar technique used in describing utopias. Two well-known examples are Edward Bellamy, *Looking Backward* (New York; New American Library, 1960/1888), and Samuel Butler, *Erewhon* (London: Penguin, 1985/1872)

Education by its very nature, should help people to develop their best selves — to become people with pleasing talents, useful and satisfying occupations, self-understanding, sound character, a host of appreciations, and a commitment to continuous learning.

Nel Noddings

III

Knowledge and Insight in Education

by P. Krishna

There is a close connection between the type of education we are imparting in society and the problems we are facing in modern society. Society is composed of individuals and its characteristics depend on the characteristics of the individuals comprising it. The individual is formed in the course of education, in which is included the education at home, in school and college and through the media. During the 20th century we have made tremendous progress outwardly and our life has changed drastically as a consequence of that. This progress is the outcome of the knowledge we have generated through our system of education. Several acute problems we were facing at the beginning of the 20th century have been solved, but newer problems have arisen. Wars have become far more dangerous as a consequence of the enhanced knowledge and power we have acquired now. The industrial revolution has caused enormous ecological imbalances about which we are reading every day. Relationships are breaking down and there seems to be greater violence and aggression in society today than we had in the past. We do not seem to have evolved significantly in our psychological makeup and human beings find it as difficult to love their neighbors today as they did a hundred years ago.

If we are facing so many problems at the end of this century of stupendous progress, then we must stop and ask ourselves what it is that we have done wrong? Why are we facing so many serious problems even though we have amassed so much knowledge, created so much power/ability and become so "intelligent"? Do we need better controls or do we need to change direction? Will more of the same kind of education as we have been imparting solve these problems? Do we need still better computers, still faster airplanes, still more goods, yet more knowledge and efficiency and will that solve the problems we have discussed above? If not, then should we not reexamine our priorities in education and question the very vision with which we have been working so far?

The Present Vision of Education

What is our vision of education today? What kind of human being are we aiming to produce? The aims may vary a little from country to country but essentially, all over the world, education is aiming to produce a human being who is intelligent, knowledgeable, hardworking, efficient, disciplined, smart, successful and hopefully a leader in his field of endeavor. If one may most humbly point out, Adolph Hitler had all these qualities and yet most people regard him as the most evil person of this century. The only thing he lacked was love and compassion. So what is there in our present day education to prevent the creation of a Hitler or of little Hitlers for that matter?

The holocaust, perhaps the greatest crime of this century, was perpetrated in a country that had the best of science, art, music and culture of the kind we are aiming to inculcate through education today. So what is there in present day education to prevent the recurrence of the holocaust? Indeed, we are perhaps at the brink of a still larger holocaust in which the whole of mankind may be eliminated from the face of the earth in a nuclear war. Present day education is basically developing greater and greater power; but both God and the Devil (as conceived by us) are infinitely powerful. Are we ensuring that the power we produce will be used in godly ways and not in devilish ways? If not, then it is irresponsible to generate power.

15

The major challenges facing mankind today are not due to a lack of education. They are not created by the illiterate villagers in Asia or Africa, they are created by highly educated and professional minds — lawyers, business administrators, scientists, economists, military commanders, diplomats and the like — who plan and run governments, organizations and businesses. So we need to look at the kind of education we are imparting and not the quantity. When you do that it becomes clear that we are producing lopsided human beings: very advanced, very clever, very capable in their intellect but almost primitive in other aspects of life; top scientists and engineers who can send human beings to the moon but who may be brutal with their spouses or their neighbors; human beings who have a vast understanding of the way the universe operates but little understanding of themselves or their life.

It is this lopsided development of the individual that is responsible for all the problems we are facing today. As educationalist we must accept that when we impart knowledge it is also our responsibility to impart or awaken the wisdom to employ it rightly. Our present day education has not paid serious attention to that responsibility. ...

The Role of Education

The human mind has several capacities and functions but our education and culture emphasize only those based on memory and thinking because of their utilitarian value. For the purpose of discussion one may categorize the various capacities of our mind into the following groups based on similarity within each group:

Group 1: Perception, observation, attention, and awareness.
Group 2: Memory, information, language, knowledge, conditioning, and instinct.
Group 3: Thinking, reasoning, planning, technique, logic, mathematics, concentration, inquiry, imagination, invention, humor, intelligence (of thought).

Group 4:   Feeling, emotion, sensitivity, sentiment, beauty, romance, art, and poetry.

Group 5:   Insight, vision, intuition, intelligence (not of thought), silence, and creativity.

One can add other functions under each group and also find many that are combinations of two or more functions listed above because the brain has the capacity to function in an integrated manner. To that extent these groups, though differentiated from each other, are not exclusive. One differentiates them for the convenience of discussion and analysis but one is also aware that all these functions taken together form one composite whole, which is our brain-mind combination. Right education should ensure a balanced development of all the functions of the mind and body; but that is not what we are doing right now, thereby creating lopsided individuals, whose mind functions acutely only in a very limited area.

We have cultivated, admired, and worshiped knowledge, memory, and the intelligence of thought, but neglected the other functions our mind is capable of. It is important to remind ourselves of the limitations of knowledge and thought, however useful these may be in our life. The scholar of Buddhist philosophy does not have the same consciousness as the Buddha although he may have a knowledge greater than that of the Buddha. One can study all the literature on nonviolence and still remain a very violent or aggressive person. The description and analysis of a poem cannot capture the actual feeling with which it was written. The description is not the described and unless one experiences the real thing, words have very little meaning. Even in the field of Science, the professor who can deduce all the equations derived by Einstein does not necessarily have the insight that Einstein had into the nature or time, space, energy, and matter. The human mind is capable of a deep and direct perception, which is quite different from the outcome of an intellectual thought process.

Ramanujam is an outstanding example of a mathematician who intuitively came upon correct answers to several problems without being able to logically think out the proof. Several great discoveries have been made through sudden flashes of insight, during which the thought process is temporarily in abeyance. For such an insight to come into being there has to be a certain freedom from the known which is totally different from ignorance. Therefore, while it is obviously necessary to impart knowledge and the skills of clear thinking, it is equally important to let the mind lie fallow and experience a deep silence in which alone there exists the possibility of an insight to occur. Keen observation, wide awareness, and a deep sense of beauty and order are all essential for this.

Our present education system, even at its best, burdens the mind of the student with too much knowledge and assiduously promotes constant and intensive thinking by rewarding him for being clever in his thought-processes. Such activity is counter-productive unless it is coupled with moments of silence, of deep reflection, and with activities that involve the slowing down of the thought process. The mind must not be constantly in a hurry or working feverishly with ambition if it is to be capable of deep perception, observation and attention. It must have time to "stand and stare." The ability to have a perceptive awareness of the entire field is as essential, if not more, than the ability to focus or concentrate one's thoughts on a fragment of the field. One must not only explore a mountain by getting close to it, but also see its beauty from afar.

The constant pressure that is put on the student by our demand for better and better achievement in examinations destroys creativity and inquiry both of which are absolutely essential for right education. Let me quote here what two great educationists of our time have had to say in this regard. Ivan Illych says in his book on *Deschooling Society,* "The pupil is schooled to confuse teaching with learning, grade-advancement with education, a diploma with competence and fluency with ability to say something new?" Elsewhere, Einstein has stated, "It is, in fact, nothing short of a miracle that the modern methods of instruction have not yet entirely strangled the holy curiosity of inquiry, for this delicate plant, aside from stimulation, stands mainly in need of freedom; without this it goes to wreck and ruin without fail?" In order to nurture talent and promote excellence it is necessary to expose a student to a wide variety of subjects and activities, help him to discover where his natural interest lies and let him pursue his intrinsic talent. The demand of parents and society to force the child into a particular course of study, such as Engineering or Medicine, and compulsorily cultivate talents in that direction is shortsighted and destructive of the natural intelligence of the child. Education with such a self-projected and limited objective is bound to produce mediocrity. It also causes a lot of psychological damage by creating conflict and inferiority in a student, which are inevitable when we expect him to fit into a preset pattern or direction.

There has been of late, a lot of talk about imparting human values in education. While this is a laudable objective if it is attempted intelligently, it can be disastrous if it is reduced to sermonizing or trying to get the students to memorize "good" thoughts. Thoughts are superficial things that can be acquired from any book, memorized and then repeated. We actually are what we feel deep down within us and not what we think. Mere knowledge of good thoughts does not create virtue; it ends up creating hypocrisy. For example, knowledge of the concept of nonviolence does not help to eliminate violence. It is only a deep understanding and awareness of the causes of violence in one's own psyche that can bring about the ending of violence and this needs a lot of observation, examination, and inquiry into oneself. Without that, to only practice nonviolence outwardly, while remaining aggressive, violent and domineering from within is not only superficial but also generates a constant conflict between what one is and what one should be. One is then not completely honest with oneself and gets caught in image building. Virtue has very little significance unless it is spontaneous. Cold, calculated and premeditated practice of virtue is really a façade behind which the real self hides itself. It is important to realize that self-knowledge cannot be acquired from books alone. One has to come upon it through constant observation of and reflection on one's thoughts and activities in every day life and in relationships. The mere acceptance of the thoughts of great people does not bring self-knowledge. It is only a deep insight into our own psyche (or self) that naturally alters our values and outlook on life, thereby cleansing our feelings at the source.

In this field it is very important for the student to learn by observing himself and to question and doubt what others have said. Unless he discovers the truth for himself it does not become a part of him. The knowledge of the truth is not the same as a direct perception of the truth and only the latter has value. Human values must therefore be taught by arousing the interest of the child and creating in him a deep sense of inquiry — not through conformity and acceptance of what others have said. In this field, even more than in others, knowledge has little value if it is not coupled with insight. It is through deep insight and inquiry that there can be a fundamental transformation in human consciousness and education needs to concern itself with bringing about such a transformation.

IV

A Cultured, Educated Life

by Swamini Saradapriyananda

Nature and culture are two distinct and separate things. We are all born with a nature of our own, a part of it common to all and part personal to each. Culture is what we acquire by education, observation, and hard practice. A person who brings out a transformation in his or her personality that results in the creation of joy and harmony all around and peace within can be said to be truly educated. When outer harmony alone is attained at the expense of inner joy, the individual suffers; hence, it is partial education only. When outer harmony is sacrificed for the sake of inner satisfaction, it is a false education and is not worthy of its name. Such a person will not have even true inner joy. Thus, education must provide a person with a way to reconcile his or her inner and outer demands.

Respect for Mother Nature

Human beings have several physical needs, such as food, clothing, and shelter, besides the natural needs for air and water. All these needs can and have to be satisfied through Mother Nature, who is ever ready to supply all the wants of all beings in the world. While animals make use of Nature as she is, human beings change and improve her to suit their superior tastes, acquired through their more evolved thinking power. Even then, plentiful and abounding Nature yields all her riches without shirking the probing intellect of the human. As a result, we see the glorious manner in which modern science has changed the face of the earth.

Such progress is no doubt the result of education. However, human beings have yet to learn something more. They should realize that Nature is a pliable material in their hands and has to be properly used, since for all time to come she is there to serve us. If we don't know how to keep Nature pure and clean, future generations will be doomed. Nature has a way of keeping herself pure from the ordinary uses of living beings, but when man with his scientific knowledge invents machinery that pollutes the air, the water, and the earth, she requires a long time to get purged of all impurities that are poured into her. In the meantime, generations of living beings get hurt by man's thoughtless inventions. So present-day education must develop in man a healthy respect toward bountiful Nature and a precaution not to take undue advantage of her wealth.

Selflessness

Another quality that education needs to foster in human beings is the ability to overcome selfishness. Narrowness of vision makes a person completely identified with his or her physical body, and all thoughts necessarily converge toward personal gain. Yet man is a social animal. He cannot live by himself like a mountain or an island. His life is bound with the general wellbeing of the society of which he is part. He has a dual existence in that he is a distinct individuality completely different from others, yet he is a part of the total also. A harmonious blending of these two forms of existence yields joy in life.

We must learn to think big — at the total level as well as the individual level. This is where true culture and the concept of righteousness come in. To destroy society for the promotion of self-interest is demoniacal; to neglect self-interest for the sake of harmony around is suicidal. A rosebush need not destroy the jasmine in order to bring forth her fragrance, nor does the rosebush need to destroy itself to keep harmony with the jasmine. Both the jasmine and the rose have a place in the Lord's good creation, and they can live together harmoniously.

A human being should be educated in getting a clear idea of what is right and what is wrong: he or she must be taught to walk the path without treading on the heels of others. Values of what is proper and improper must be taught to him as part of education.

These values are no doubt being taught in the schools and colleges by way of good manners and social behavior, but judging from the results, it is clear that this teaching is not enough. It is not enough to preach to a person that he should not be selfish without giving him a deeper insight as to what happens if he does not follow that injunction.

Man is considered the roof and crown of all creation, even though he is physically weaker than many of the lower creation and is not provided with Nature's natural protection, which the lower beings have. Man holds this position because of the level of his psychic evolution. Though his physical body has as many demands as those of the lower beings, he can detach himself from those demands when he is emotionally moved or intellectually inspired. This detachment from the physical body is his glory. It is this trait that has to be cultivated and developed through education.

The body should be given the minimum that is necessary to keep it healthy; no luxuries or undue comforts need to pamper it. Plain living and high thinking are the signs of true education.

The Purpose of Education

The correct way of life can be taught only when there is correct knowledge of what education is meant for. Most parents and students know only of one purpose of education: to learn a skill so money can be earned. However, education and profession are two different things. The purpose of education is to make man civilized and cultured, while the purpose of a profession is to provide a means for earning one's livelihood. Uneducated and illiterate people can earn money. The delinking of education from its money-earning worth is urgently required, since the linking of the two, clouds all other better sentiments in the educational field today. The unhealthy rush in some professional colleges today is driven more by the desire to accumulate money-earning power than by the aptitude or natural skill of the students.

A correct idea about life and the nature of experiences that come to us in life has to be taught as part of our education. All people seek joy. They make sincere efforts to get it, and yet only a few lucky ones appear to find joy. What are the forces that govern the law of experiences? Some of us have a vague idea of the law of action: "You reap as you sow" — that is to say, we deserve what we desire. This is reasonable and logical. Most of us have no difficulty in appreciating this idea. But we are often puzzled to see that the law appears to fail. We find that in life many hardworking people, many good people, suffer for no apparent cause. It is also common knowledge that many bad and evil people appear to be very successful and enjoy the fruit of their evil actions. What happens to the doctrine of action? Unable to understand the mysterious workings of action, many people let go of their principles and take to shortcut methods to gain joy in life.

This is where the educational system has to step in to give true and correct knowledge of the workings of the law of action. Life is not a single phenomenon, beginning with the birth of the body and ending with its death. The birth and death of a body constitute one wave that rises and falls in the total existence of an individual, and each such wave is a link between past and future lives. The cumulative effect of all that has been done up to the last life produces the present life, whose momentum and direction have already been determined before it commenced. Whatever we do now can only add its effects for the future and not for the present. Hence, the present life is a chance to formulate our future life. We have to accept the present and plan for the future. If this is properly understood, most of us would save many a sigh over spilt milk. A spirit of resignation in the present and a grim determination for the future will automatically follow.

Finally, education should include true understanding of what the goal of life is. Every science starts its investigations with the many and points to one underlying truth behind the many: Physics talks of one energy that expresses itself as many forces. Chemistry talks of the existence of an entity called matter, which expresses itself as a variety of substances. Botany and biology indicate that all plant life and animal life are truly one. So, too, to know that one supreme Consciousness is the true nature of all beings is the highest achievement of humankind. Life is a journey undertaken to learn this truth. Once we have understood this truth, we will no longer have to struggle to learn anything more. This Oneness is the destination of all life. Once we realize it, we will end our ignorance about the purpose of life and will not waste our energies in futile and vain pursuits. Life is too precious to be frittered away in unnecessary digressions. The wise man knows how to choose the straight path toward the final consummation of life.

This is not to say that life becomes a serious, morose affair devoid of all fun and joy. The opposite is true. When a piece of delicate machinery is properly used for the purpose for which it was invented, it yields satisfaction to the user. A car is meant for travel. The driver should know two things: how to handle the car and what course to follow to reach his destination. If the driver does not know how to handle the car or is not familiar with the traffic rules, he will get in trouble. If he knows how to drive and understands the traffic rules, his journey will be comfortable. Still, if he does not know his destination, he will never finish the journey satisfactorily. The going can become long and tiresome; perhaps he will never reach his destination at all.

So too, when we know the purpose of life, we can handle the delicate machinery called the human personality and can steer it through life without clashing with the people and world around us. Such a life becomes a cultured life, an educated one.

V

The Ancient Wisdom
of Education

by Swami Ishwarananda

[Based on discourses at Chinmaya Mission Chicago, February 2006.]

Knowledge is the backbone of a culture while common sense is the backbone for civilization. Culture refines a person from within, while common sense disciplines a person externally. Education is the means for both knowledge and common sense. The mentors, sources, and means of education vary from culture to culture. In the ancient Hindu society, a teacher played the role of a mentor, a godfather, and a spiritual guide to inspire the students who lived with him. Lord Rama and Lord Krishna, though incarnations of the Absolute Truth, also received instructions from their teachers, only to exemplify the Vedic wisdom "he who has a teacher, gains wisdom" (*ācāryvān puruṣo veda*).

One of the well-known young students of the ancient wisdom was Nachiketa from the *Kaṭhopaniṣad*. (The *Kaṭhopaniṣad* is one of the ten classical Upanishads.) The Sanskrit meaning of Nachiketa is, "he who has no doubt." He was an ardent student, who sought wisdom from *Yama* — the Lord of Death. The Lord granted him three boons. For the first boon, Nachiketa sought the peace and welfare of his father, who was sorrow-stricken when Nachiketa left him at home. For the second boon, he requested Lord of Death to give him the knowledge of the ritual that can lead him to heaven. When instructed and guided by a competent teacher, even a dull student would excel. Nachiketa who was faithfully brilliant and passionless could repeat the instructions without any flaw. His mind was innocent but inquisitive. His third boon was a doubt: "Is there life after death? If so, what is it and how is it?" A significant portion of the *Kaṭhopaniṣad* text is dedicated to answer this question of the ardent student. True to his name, Nachiketa finally emerged as a wise person with his doubts cleared, ignorance removed, and *karma* reduced. In his commentary on the *Kaṭhopaniṣad,* the great master of *Advaita* philosophy, Adi Shankaracharya, indicates various aspects of ancient ways of education. Following is an analysis in the modern context.

Three Mentors of Education

Johann Goethe once said, "Everywhere, we learn only from those whom we love." Education begins at home with two mentors — the mother and the father. The language of love is the mother tongue. Through her love, the mother guides the child to emulate culture and tradition. Even a calf does not know how to drink milk without the mother cow, which helps the calf to learn. The father teaches conduct and discipline, without which no accomplishment will last. He prepares the child for the dawn of higher wisdom just as the planter ploughs the land before sowing the seed.

The formal teacher is the third mentor, who inspires the student for the rest of his life. He gives required insight to investigate and differentiate Truth from False; he opens the eye of wisdom to navigate oneself from darkness to light and also strengthens the faith to transcend from death to immortality.

A well-known Sanskrit verse says: "Cloth, body, speech, knowledge, and humility — he who lacks (even one of) these five does not command respect." The first three are the contributions of the parents and the remaining two, which provide fulfillment in life, are by a formal teacher.

SWAMI ISHWARANANDA

Three Sources of Education

Many an ignorant person thinks that mere knowledge is education. The first vice-president and second president of democratic India, Dr. Sarvepalli Radhakrishnan, once said in a convocation address at the University of Madras: "Dear students, congratulations for your graduation. Go out into the world and get educated!" Life teaches us more than books. Yet, we cannot completely rule out the role of the books. The documented experiences and wisdom of the wise are the books. In the traditional system of education in India, the Vedas, *Smṛti*, and advice of the wise are considered as the three significant sources of education.

The Vedas and *Smṛti* are called scriptures. Scriptures are those that have information which is unalterable. The four Vedas — *Ṛg, Yajur, Sāma,* and *Atharva* — are also known as *Śruti* — recorded version of what was "heard" by the realized masters. They conveyed their wisdom only by words and not by any written document. Retaining the spoken words and following the memorized instructions was the life of a disciple, who lived with strict discipline in the abode of the formal teacher. In the course of time, when such a system of education was replaced by a school system, written documents became unavoidable. *Smṛti*, such as the *Yajñavālkya Smṛti* and *Manu Smṛti*, are the documents of the later masters who documented their experiences based on the inspirations they derived from the Vedas.

An educator should reinforce his teachings with personal wisdom. In the absence of such sincere personal application, perpetuation of correct knowledge will be at stake. In the absence of familiarity with *Śruti* and *Smṛti*, one should gather knowledge and seek advice from the wise, who have gained a right perspective of life through their own personal contemplation.

Three Methods of Education

Education is incomplete if the student does not obtain clarity in thinking and faith in his or her personal development. In the ancient system of India, three methods of education were used. They are: Perceptual, Inferential, and Documental evidence. Perceptual is the objective method of education which includes theory followed by experimentation. Inferential is the logical method of education, which requires a conceptual understanding supported by rational thinking.

The uniqueness of the ancient system lies in the third method — documental evidence. The tenth planet which today's scientists have discovered was there even before the discovery of the highly sophisticated telescope! The telescope only revealed what was present but unknown. Similarly education through faith in documental evidence is about that which cannot be easily grasped by the range of the intellect. This provided humility and wonderment in the minds of the students, who revered the creation and creative force. Faith in the unknown also kindled the adventurous spirit in the young minds to explore the unknown through ardent meditation.

Education should not stop at the school or the university or on obtaining a lucrative profession. Unfortunately, the kind of education provided by the universities today stops at perceptual and inferential levels and does not give room for the third method. Learning about the unknown through documental evidence at early stages of education helps one to live life with a purpose to realize the unknown.

Three Applications of Education

Learning any knowledge is not merely for blind reproduction. Nor is learning only for earning! Education should provide maturity to a person to help him rise above imperfections caused by lower attachments. In the Vedic system of education the foremost instruction to the student was to practice daily sacrifice or *yajña*. The teacher was an inspiration who lived a life of sacrifice — selflessly working for the common good. Emulating this value from the teacher, a mature student applied his knowledge only to bring prosperity to everyone around him through which he perfected purity in action.

Continuous self-study and dissemination are the second set of instructions of the teacher, which helped the student never to become proud of his education. The vast wealth of knowledge we find in the scriptures were contributed by those who were ever eager to find out more than what their eyes could see and ears could hear! A Sanskrit verse illustrates this very well: "O Goddess of Learning, your treasure is unusual; the more it is spent, the more it increases; if one stores it, it becomes extinct!"

Sharing one's wealth with others is the third application of education. Where wealth is hoarded, the Goddess of Learning departs. Hoarding wealth creates fear, lack of love, and bondage. In the Hindu tradition, education is compared to a river — Saraswati, which symbolically indicates the continuous flow. The flow should end only in the ocean. Education should end only in Enlightenment!

Ralph Waldo Emerson said: "Knowledge is the antidote to fear." Nachiketa is the most evident proof for this. His conversation with death to obtain the appropriate knowledge made him free, fearless, and enlightened. The final verse of *Kaṭhopaniṣad* assures us, "anyone else too who becomes a knower of wisdom attains enlightenment." (II:3.18)

PART TWO

Parents and Environment

School never ends. The classroom is everywhere.

Anna Quindlen

The child's education begins the moment it sees the light of day. It can even be said that it begins in the mother's womb. Whatever habits of thought, action, and feeling are formed in a man's early days last throughout his life. A man's moral structure is sown in his childhood, though he is likely to be influenced by good and bad contacts in his early youth and manhood. If a child receives wholesome impressions in his early days, he is likely to be influenced by good contacts in youth and manhood.

If the growth of a child begins in the right manner, that is the most important step towards the consummation of the excellence of which his tender nature is capable. The surroundings of a child provide efficient means for his education and good instruction. A child learns his first notions of the world around him from his mother, from his immediate surroundings and his playmates. He should be trained to arouse his keen, fresh perception to observe rightly, to record correctly, to infer justly, and to express cogently.

Swami Sivananda

VI

Imparting Values
by Swami Chinmayananda

[The following article is from a recorded conversation between students and Swami Chinmayananda.]

Meera: Do you think that strict moral training from a very early age will curb the urge to evil? What kind of moral education should be imparted to a child from the primary level, so that he or she will be spontaneously good and not have to go through repeated moral conflicts while making a choice?

Jyoti: How can we best express to our children the idea of genuine values so that they grow up with open minds, not with a once and for all acceptance but with the ability to sift and decide on right values? If we impart a vague sense of values they may grow up having no real sense of them at all. On the other hand, if we decide for them, they may be limited in their approach to values.

Swamiji: The first question is answered by the second question. The first question is: How are we to do it? The moral part only comes once the activity starts and we classify activities as moral and immoral. Now, how am I to make an individual to act morally? By giving him healthy values. Values of life determine how the individual reacts to the external world and finally expresses it.

Jyoti: How can one impart the values?

Swamiji: Imparting values must be started from the very beginning. Values are so subtle that even an elderly person will not be able to conceive the idea unless it is concretized in an individual acting those values in a given set of specific conditions.

This is the method. In our modern education we don't give the children any ideal. Data is given but no ideal to pursue. Ideals must be given. The story is not for history; it is for imparting an ideal. Give it to them and they will always check whether their action was morally good or not, beautiful or not. These children will grow up and in their togetherness will constitute the society.

The social behavior in any part of the world, in any period of time, will be the sum total work of the team of people that constitute the society. Each individual functions in the world outside ordered by, and governed by his thoughts. The quality and the nature of the thoughts are determined by what values the individual respects. If the values respected by the individuals are wrong, the individual's activities can never be good. Similarly, if the values entertained by the community is wrong, their total behavior will only be bringing more and more sorrow to them. Hence in the modern times we are insisting upon value-based education. The healthy values, psychologically healthy for the individual and therefore healthy for the community have been experimented upon and given out as moral and ethical principles.

Bur first, we have to conceive and understand and appreciate these values. Thereafter, a mere possession is not sufficient. Each individual should learn to live up to them. Culture cannot be taught, it has to be caught. In order to impart these to our growing children there is no way other than concretizing these values through the heroic stories of people who have lived these values ... hence, the need for stories. The mythological stories of India are perfect and artistic examples on how to impart these values to children. Never can children's education be complete unless we impart to them a true appreciation of the eternal values of life and also help them to open up their sense of beauty and rhythm, their aestheticism and ethicism. That is the reason why we not only try to mold them with our stories of heroism and excellence in character but also give them a free choice to discover and develop their inner secret talents for music, dance, painting, and so forth. It has been found very rewarding in all our educational centers.

Children are the architects of the future world. They are the builders of humanity. The seed of spiritual values should be sown in the young hearts, and the condition should be made favorable for its sprouting and steady growth by the exercise of proper control and discipline. Cared for with the warmth of love and affection, such a tree shall blossom forth flowers of brotherhood, universal love, peace, bliss, beauty and perfection.

Since time immemorial, the great acharyas of Hindu culture considered that "Our children are our wealth," and rightly so. The formative period of childhood is the most malleable state of mind when an individual is available for molding and casting into a right personality.

To mold the behavior of an individual is to mold character for the community. This is what education strives to achieve. I believe that we can give a purposeful direction to a personality even in the days of its almost unconscious early childhood. Later on, no doubt, we must hammer out for the child new extensions and open up new dimensions for its play in the society through literary, scientific, and social studies. Whatever the child is to be later on — say a political leader, an economist, philosopher, scientist, or a glorious artist — his contribution to the society will directly depend on his character and personality.

The state needs the mystic and the poet, the musician and the artist, no less than the scientist and the businessman, the teacher and the soldier. Whether he is a mystic, or a soldier, one must have character. Or else, he is not a blessing to the state; he will prove himself to be only an ulcer on the body politic.

Swami Chinmayananda

VII

Raising an Unhurried Child
by Carl Honoré

> The most effective kind of education is that a child should
> play amongst lovely things.
>
> *Plato (427-347 BC)*

Harry Lewis is dean of the undergraduate school at Harvard. In early 2001, he attended a meeting at which students were invited to air their grievances about staff at the Ivy League university. One undergraduate kicked up a memorable fuss. He wanted to double major in Biology and English, and cram all the work into three, instead of the usual four, years. He was exasperated with his academic advisor, who was unable, or unwilling, to devise a schedule to accommodate all the courses. As he listened to the student moan about being held back, Lewis felt a light bulb flash above his head.

"I remember thinking, 'Wait a minute, you need help, but not in the way you think you do,'" says the dean. "You need to take time to think about what is really important, rather than trying to figure out how to pack as much as you can into the shortest possible schedule."

After the meeting, Lewis began to reflect on how the twenty-first-century student has become a disciple of hurry. From there it was a short step to speaking out against the scourge of overstuffed schedules and accelerated degree programs. In the summer of 2001, the dean wrote an open letter to every first-year undergraduate at Harvard. It was an impassioned plea for a new approach to life on campus and beyond. It was also a neat précis of the ideas that lie at the heart of the Slow philosophy. The letter, which now goes out to Harvard freshmen every year, is entitled: *Slow Down.*

Over seven pages, Lewis makes the case for getting more out of university — and life — by doing less. He urges students to think twice before racing through their degrees. It takes time to master a subject, he says, pointing out that top medical, law and business schools increasingly favor mature candidates with more to offer than an "abbreviated and intense undergraduate education." Lewis warns against piling on too many extracurricular activities. What is the point, he asks, of playing lacrosse, chairing debates, organizing conferences, acting in plays and editing a section of the campus newspaper if you end up spending your whole Harvard career in overdrive, striving not to fall behind schedule? Much better to do fewer things and have time to make the most of them.

When it comes to academic life, Lewis favors the same less-is-more approach. Get plenty of rest and relaxation, he says, and be sure to cultivate the art of doing nothing. "Empty time is not a vacuum to be filled," writes the dean. "It is the thing that enables the other things on your mind to be creatively rearranged, like the empty square in the 4x4 puzzle that makes it possible to move the other fifteen pieces around." In other words, doing nothing, being Slow, is an essential part of good thinking.

Slow Down is not a charter for slackers and born-again beatniks. Lewis is as keen on hard work and academic success as the next Harvard heavyweight. His point is simply that a little selective slowness can help students to live and work better. "In advising you to think about slowing down and limiting your structured activities, I do not mean to discourage you from high achievement, indeed from the pursuit of extraordinary excellence," he concludes. "But you are more likely to sustain the intense effort needed to accomplish first-rate work in one area if you allow yourself some leisure time, some recreation, some time for solitude." ...

The Freedom to Slow Down

Today, educators and parents around the world are once again taking steps to allow young people the freedom to slow down, to be children. In my search for interviewees, I post messages on a few parenting websites. Within days, my inbox is crammed with emails from three continents. Some are from teenagers lamenting their haste-ridden lives. An Australian girl named Jess describes herself as a "rushed teen" and tells me "I have no time for anything!" But most of the emails come from parents enthusing about the various ways their kids are decelerating.

Let's start in the classroom, where pressure is mounting for a Slower approach to learning. At the end of 2002, Maurice Holt, professor emeritus of education at the University of Colorado, Denver, published a manifesto calling for a worldwide movement for "Slow Schooling." Like others, he draws his inspiration from Slow Food. In Holt's view, stuffing information into children as fast as possible is as nourishing as wolfing down a Big Mac. Much better to study at a gentle pace, taking time to explore subjects deeply, to make connections, to learn how to think rather than how to pass exams. If eating Slow excites the palate, learning Slow can broaden and invigorate the mind.

"At a stroke, the notion of the slow school destroys the idea that schooling is about cramming, testing, and standardizing experience," Holt writes. "The slow approach to food allows for discovery, for the development of connoisseurship. Slow food festivals feature new dishes and new ingredients. In the same way, slow schools give scope for invention and response to cultural change, while fast schools just turn out the same old burgers."

Holt and his supporters are not extremists. They do not want children to learn less, or to spend the school day goofing around. Hard work has a place in a Slow classroom. Instead of obsessing over tests, targets and timetables, though, kids would be given the freedom to fall in love with learning. Rather than spend a history lesson listening to a teacher spewing dates and facts about the Cuban missile crisis, a class might hold its own UN-style debate. Each pupil would research the position of a major country on the 1962 standoff, and then make the case to the rest of the class. The children still work hard, but without the drudgery of rote learning. Like every other wing of the Slow movement, "Slow Schooling" is about balance. Countries that take a Slower approach to education are already reaping the benefits.

VIII

Parenting

by Swami Tejomayananda

From the standpoint of Vedanta, everyone belongs to God. Therefore, while raising children we should not forget this very important fact. I belong to God because I am part of God, and everyone else belongs to God in the same way. As parents we are only providing material for the physical body, not the individual self (*jīva*.) A *jīva* comes into this world of its own accord *to fulfill some kind of destiny.* Everyone has come into this world in the same manner. We have all come with a purpose to fulfill. It just so happens that we are together in the same family, but each person has a very distinct reason and purpose to be here.

For instance, if we travel by plane or train, we do not know who our co-passengers are until we get onto the plane. The only thing common to all passengers is that they wanted to travel on the same day, and on the same flight. They are all together because of a common karma. But if you ask them individually as to where they are going and why they are going, everyone has a different answer. They all travel for different reasons, some are going on a vacation, others to attend a marriage or a funeral, while another one may be going for an interview.

Similarly, some common karma brings a family together, a mother, a father, and children. We meet people in life, spend some time together, and share the good and the bad. Then like fellow travelers, we get off at different places and go our own way. Therefore, let's remove the "I-ness" and "my-ness," from life; my child, my father, my mother, and my friend, and look at it from a more objective standpoint.

Khalil Gibran in his book *The Prophet*, states that the children "come through you, they don't belong to you," like the arrow, which comes through the bow but does not belong to the bow; it just follows its own course.

In the *Bhagavad Gītā* Lord Krishna says: "I am the Mother and the Father and the Grandfather of this universe." (9:17) The Lord is saying, why do you parents think that you have become the mother and father? The Lord is the Father, and we all belong to Him. With this understanding, our vision becomes clear, and our way of looking at any situation will change. We all come across situations in life where the outcome surprises us. When we conduct our Vedanta training course, many people ask, "Swamiji, how are the students (*brahmacārī*) shaping up? Who do you think is the most promising person?" Sometimes the most promising one quits, and the one appearing to be the least promising will outshine by the end. It is really strange, so I have stopped judging. Let only the Lord judge. Why should I judge?

Our Role

Let us now consider our role as parents. Our role should be rooted in the fact that we belong to God, and in the entire scheme of things, each of us is an instrument in the hands of the Lord. Yet the Lord in His compassion gives everyone an opportunity to achieve something.

We need to understand that each of us is part (*aṁśa*) of the Lord. The real Mother and Father of the entire Universe is the Lord. The great saint, Swami Ramdas, said that there is only the Lord and his Nature. Where did the third entity "I" come from? Our role is that of an instrument. We are not the doer, but only an instrument doing what the doer wants us to do. The doer is the Lord. In *Upadeśa Sāra*, Ramana Maharshi says in the very first verse: "By the command of the Creator of the world, the fruits of action are gained."

Slowly we come to realize that as parents we play the role of an instrument. The Lord has given us a chance to be the mother or father of a given child. But we know that this child belongs to the Lord, and we also belong to the Lord. Now what is the best thing that we as parents can do for this child? Swami Chinmayananda has said that your role is like that of a farmer or a gardener. You do not create the seed. You do not create the soil. The potential power is already in the seed. You do not inject anything in the seed. The role of a farmer, an agriculturist, or a gardener is to prepare the soil properly, then to sow the seeds at the right time, and to give them the required amount of water, shade, sunlight — in short, to provide conducive environment for the seeds to grow. If the seeds have something in them, they will sprout. But if the seeds themselves are roasted, or if the soil is not proper, or there is too much rain, or too little, then what can the gardener do? Therefore, in the first place, the seed has to have the potential to grow into something. Then there are other necessary conducive factors. Our effort is only one of the contributory factors, but it is the totality of this world that really acts on the seed. Therefore, remember that the result of the efforts (*karma phala*) do not come because of our action alone. Our duty is to provide the right atmosphere in a given situation and if the seed has potential, it will grow.

If you have put forth all your efforts and expected results do not unfold, then you are not to be blamed. Your conscience will be clear that you have done all that you could do. This is true, not only in reference to parenting, but for every activity in life.

When your children are born, it is your job to give them food, clothing, shelter, and education. But along with education, we also have to give them good culture, namely the *Samskaaras* — the impressions that will prompt them to make right choices and blossom. Many times parents, who want their children to be cultured, send them to our classes for children — called "Bal Vihar." The parents say, "You go to B.V., we will watch T.V.!" So they want culture only for their children, and not for themselves. A family should grow together. There is a well-known saying: "A family that prays together, stays together." When parents and children are all together, their vision is the same and they can live together harmoniously.

Setting an Example

Many times parents are concerned about teaching their children while they themselves are ignorant about their own culture. We must begin with ourselves. Sometimes parents ask me, "Swami-ji, when should we start teaching our values and culture to our children?" I tell them, "Before the child is born." Those values should already be in you; only then will your child imbibe them. The child starts his learning process while he or she is in the mother's womb. That is the rationale behind prenatal education. Our scriptures also believe in this, they say that pregnant women should imbibe only things that are of noble nature, since what they think and do is passed on to the child.

Swami Chinmayananda used to speak about this subject in a very outspoken and humorous way. He said that some mothers watch wild programs on TV during pregnancy. They go to all sorts of parties and take part in dancing, drinking, and singing. Therefore when the baby is born, he or she also comes out whistling! Imparting culture to our children is the most important thing. But we must begin with ourselves. That's why Swamiji said, "Culture cannot be taught, it can only be caught." When children watch their parents, they automatically copy. The culture, therefore, has to be in us so that it can be passed on to our children.

Preparing for Parenthood

One problem is our own ignorance. The other problem is that we have not prepared ourselves properly for the job of parenting. For many parents the child comes as a surprise, they seem to be caught unaware, and they are not prepared for parenthood.

Do you remember how much you prepared in school or college before your annual examination? Even now, when we go for an interview, we prepare. But, when it comes to living our entire life, there is no preparation. The reason life has become a problem is that we are so ill prepared. We need to understand the entire picture. We should try to provide an atmosphere for the children so that they can grow imbibing these values. Many times parents themselves cannot give values. This is where scriptural teaching through some teacher comes in or attending family spiritual camps.

Earlier I hinted upon one point, that if we want our children to be good, intelligent, cultured, and respectful, we will have to begin by developing the same qualities in ourselves. The *Gita* clearly says: "People follow the leader." Whatever standard is set by the elders or the leaders, the rest of the people follow it. History has shown us that when a king became a Buddhist, his subjects also followed Buddhism.

There is a famous statement: "As the King, so the subjects." This does not only apply to kings but to every one of us. A father or a mother is the leader, a role model for the child. Therefore, we must keep in mind, that if we want the children to follow a particular ideal or a way of living, then we must ourselves live that way. Otherwise, we are living a contradiction amounting to hypocrisy.

IX

Complete Education

by the Mother
(Sri Aurobindo Ashram)

The education of a human being should begin at his very birth and continue throughout his life. Indeed, if the education is to have its maximum result, it must begin even before birth: it is the mother herself who proceeds with this education by means of a twofold action, first, upon herself for her own improvement, and second, upon the child which she is forming within her physically. For it is certain that the nature of the child about to be born will depend very much upon the mother who forms it, upon her aspiration and will, as much as upon the material surroundings in which she lives. The part of education which the mother has to go through is to see that her thoughts are always beautiful and pure, her feelings always noble and fine, her material surroundings as harmonious as possible and full of a great simplicity. And if, in addition, she has a conscious and definite will to form the child according to the highest ideal she can conceive, then the very best conditions are provided for the child to come into the world with the maximum of possibilities. How many difficult efforts and useless complications are avoided thereby!

Education to be complete must have five principal aspects relating to the five principal activities of the human being: the physical, the vital, the mental, the psychic, and the spiritual. Usually, these phases of education succeed each other in a chronological order following the growth of the individual; this, however, does not mean that the one should replace the other, but that all must continue, completing each other until the end of life. ...

The majority of parents, for various reasons, take very little thought of a true education to be given to their children. When they have brought a child into the world, and when they have given him food and satisfied his various material wants by looking more or less carefully to the maintenance of his health, they think they have fully discharged their duty. Later on, they would put him in school and hand over to the teacher the care of his education.

There are other parents who know that their children should receive education and try to give it. But very few among them, even among those who are most serious and sincere, know that the first thing to do in order to be able to educate the child is to educate oneself, to become conscious and a master of oneself so that one does not set a bad example for one's child. For it is through example that education becomes effective. To say good words, give wise advice to a child has very little effect if one does not show by one's living example the truth of what one teaches. Sincerity, honesty, straight-forwardness, courage, disinterestedness, unselfishness, patience, endurance, persever-ance, peace, calm, self-control are all things that are taught infinitely better by example than by beautiful speeches. Parents, you should have a high ideal and act always in accordance with that ideal. You will see little by little your child reflecting this idea in him and manifesting spontaneously the qualities you wish to see expressed in his nature. Quite naturally a child has respect and admiration for his parents; unless they are quite unworthy, they will appear always to their children as demigods whom they will seek to imitate as well as they can.

Be Worthy of Respect

With very few exceptions, parents do not take into account the disastrous influence their defects, impulses, weaknesses, want of self-control have on their children. If you wish to be respected by your child, have respect for yourself and be at every moment worthy of respect. Never be arbitrary, despotic, impatient, ill-tempered. When your child asks you a question, do not answer him by a stupidity or a foolishness, under the pretext that he cannot understand you. You can always make yourself understood if you take sufficient pains with it, and in spite of the popular saying that it is not always good to tell the truth, I affirm that it is always good to tell the truth, only the art consists in telling it in such a way as to make it accessible to the brain of the hearer. In early life, till he is twelve or fourteen, the child's mind is hardly accessible to abstract notions and general ideas. And yet you can train it to understand these things by using images or symbols or parables. Up to a sufficiently advanced age and for some who mentally remain always children, a narrative, a story, a tale told well teaches much more than a heap of theoretical explanations.

Another pitfall to avoid: do not scold your child except with a definite purpose and only when quite unavoidable. A child scolded too often gets hardened to rebuke and no longer attaches much importance to words or severity of tone. Particularly take care not to rebuke him for a fault that you yourself commit. Children are very keen and clear-sighted observers; they soon find out your weaknesses and note them without pity.

When a child has made a mistake, see that he confesses it to you spontaneously and frankly; and when he has confessed, make him understand with kindness and affection what was wrong in his movement and that he should not repeat it. In any case, never scold him; a fault confessed must be forgiven. You should not allow any fear to slip between you and your child; fear is a disastrous way to education: invariably it gives birth to dissimulation and falsehood. Only an affection that is discerning, firm yet gentle, and a sufficient practical knowledge will create bonds of trust that are indispensable for you to make the education of your child effective. And never forget that you have to surmount yourself always and constantly so as to be at the height of your task and truly fulfill the duty that you owe your child by the mere fact of your having brought him into existence.

X

Parents as Teachers

by H. Stephen Glenn and Michael L. Brock

Isn't it often said that parents are children's first teachers? Yes, it is ... and yes, we are. But what does that mean? Does being our child's first teacher mean that it is primarily our job to teach our child the alphabet, the numbers, and how to write his or her name? Or that we are responsible to explain government and the workings of photosynthesis? Or does it mean instead that parents, by virtue of *being* parents, will be their children's teachers in the course of the daily experiences of life? An important key lies in the phrase *in the course of everyday life experiences.*

In the course of the everyday experiences of life, parents do in fact teach. We teach values through our modeling and through our cautioning. Through our interactions with other adults and children — shopping, working, visiting at family and neighborhood gatherings, attending our place of worship — we teach interpersonal skills.

We teach sensitivity or insensitivity, tolerance or intolerance, patience or impatience, self-discipline or impulsiveness, empathy or judgmentalism, and a vast array of emotions and life skills through what we model and encourage in our children as we face life's daily challenges. We teach organization skills by our actions and when we encourage children's desire to collect and sort things, help them learn to clean their rooms and put away their toys, and involve them in household chores.

We teach grammar, again through our modeling and exhortation. Michael's mother, for example, worked heroically to teach him to say "I saw it" instead of "I seen it." Once she even had him repeat "I saw it" one thousand times. (To this day he still takes pleasure in getting a rise out of her by saying "I seen it!")

We can teach math while cooking, preparing meals, and setting the dinner table ("Please measure a half-cup of milk for me." "How many knives, forks, and spoons will we need?"), while shopping at the grocery store ("This is a small orange. Pick out three that are larger."), and while paying the bills ("How much will we have left in the account if we buy that soccer ball?").

We can teach history and geography while conversing about our own family heritage, walking through our neighborhood, and traveling around our country. If American history is little more than the study of immigration, as President Kennedy suggested in one of his more famous quotes, then how could that be explained better than through discussions of our own family history? We can teach by sharing stories of how our ancestors left their homelands (whether yesterday or a thousand years ago), why they came to America, where they first settled, where they migrated, and how they contributed.

No classroom lesson on mountains and valleys, cities and country-sides, oceans and deserts, or forests and plains can compete with the knowledge children gain while driving across America. (As Michael said, "Nothing I learned about mountains and valleys in elementary school prepared me for my first experience driving over the Rockies!")

We can help children become open to the wonderful world of science by taking advantage of what we come into contact with on a daily basis. We can teach them astronomy and earth science by talking about the sun and the moon, the stars and the planets, the seasons of the year, and the rocks and stones they pick up, climb over, and scrape their knees on.

We teach biology when we answer their many questions about animals and plants they see in the neighborhood or in the zoo. We encourage them to discover basic principles of science on their own by avoiding our temptation to fill their rooms with the latest toys advertised on television and instead provide them with resources of creative play — empty boxes, blocks, geometric shapes (cubes, spheres, inclined planes, arches, pillars, and so on), string, clay, and paper.

We help children broaden their horizons, expand their awareness of their world; provide further opportunities for their natural curiosity; and open their minds to a more ready acceptance of what they will learn in school when we take them to libraries, museums, live performances, parks, historical monuments, and different natural environments. We enhance their "cultural literacy" (a critical factor in developing reading skills, according to E. D. Hirsch, best-selling author of *Cultural Literacy: What Every American Needs to Know* [Vintage Books]) when we read them stories about the men and women, places and events, music and arts, and myths and legends that comprise the American experience.

We can teach the names of things we encounter in the world. We can teach table manners and communication skills. In short, we teach continuously, naturally, and informally—*in the course of our daily activities together.* We teach without a formal classroom, without a standard curriculum, and without formal teaching aids. (And, interestingly, even without special television or videotaped learning programs, "educational toys," or trips to theme parks.) Our teaching flows naturally from our parenting. The more natural it is, the more successful it will be. ...

Self-Esteem

The importance of self-esteem cannot be overemphasized. But what is it? Where does it come from? What are its limitations? Healthy self-esteem is not arrogance or self-centeredness; it is, instead, this perception: "I am worthy of dignity and respect, not because of anything I have done or not done, but just because I am."

Self-esteem does not come from others' praise, well-meaning though it may be, or from gold stars that teachers place on papers. It emerges from experiences, both positive and negative, through which we gain wisdom and learn that we are capable, significant people who make choices that influence our lives.

Recycling an old saying, it might not be too simplistic to say that your self-esteem ends where my self-esteem begins. If my self-esteem encourages me to go out into the world with confidence and be of service to others, it is healthy. If it leads me to believe and act as though the entire world revolves around my every want and need it can be quite unhealthy.

Several years ago, a new mayor of New York City was inaugurated in a much-publicized, media-highlighted, and, ultimately, very embarrassing ceremony. With his ten-year-old son standing next to him, the new mayor began his inauguration speech.

To the embarrassment of all (except, so it appeared, to the mayor himself) and to the delight of the late-night talk shows that satirized the event during subsequent weeks, the young son proceeded to mimic his father's words, mug the camera, and gesture theatrically, all to a national television audience.

The boy behaved as one who was raised to believe that his wants and needs predominate over everything else. He behaved as one whose self-esteem is so high that the needs of the rest of the world (for solemnity and formality, not to mention plain good manners, in that case) don't count.

"High" vs. "Healthy"

For years we have heard that self-esteem is the most important issue in parenting, that by focusing on raising our children's self-esteem, everything else will work out just fine. However, it is possible to have such high, unhealthy self-esteem that we live a life of delusion. It is also possible to have low, healthy self-esteem and be living a life of humility.

If our current understanding of self-esteem doesn't translate to respect for the needs of others and realistic assessment of one's own behavior, then the issue of self-esteem needs review.

And it is finally receiving review. Thanks to critical thinkers like Alfie Kohn, author of *Punished by Rewards: The Trouble with Gold Stars, Incentive Plans, A's, Praise, and Other Bribes*, the whole self-esteem movement is being subjected to closer inspection. In a December 1994 article in the professional education journal *Kappan,* Kohn summarizes his concern about the direction the self-esteem movement has taken in these jarringly honest words: "*I'm* special, *I'm* important, here's how *I* feel about things. The whole enterprise could be said to encourage a self-absorption bordering on narcissism."

Those schooled in the issues surrounding self-esteem have long questioned the direction of the self-esteem movement in America. Two concerns regarding the directions the movement has taken are of particular note.

The first, identified by Kohn in the above quote, concerns the egocentric nature of the vocabulary of self-esteem. *I'm* special; *I'm* important. How important is it that we reinforce this with children and students? Kohn asks. Would it not be healthier to teach that we are all special, we are *all* important?

Of course, both concepts are important. Perhaps the central question is: Is it possible to de-emphasize the latter in our enthusiasm to promote the former? The example of the new mayor's son suggests that this may be happening.

The second concern, identified by many commentators on the issue, revolves around the source of self-esteem. When their sense of self is primarily developed externally (as a result of approval given by others or achieving things others value, for example), people become dependent on others and on circumstances for their sense of well-being. When sense of self is developed internally (the result of risks taken, hardships endured, personal goals met, and a sense of self-respect and self-efficacy), people can transcend the approval of others and the effects of circumstances to create their own sense of well-being.

Since the latter is clearly the healthiest and most desirable, what role do adults play in providing activities, opportunities, and challenges for young people through which they can develop healthy self-esteem? What does this view say about the wisdom of allowing children to experience discomfort and even failure so they can learn to rise above adversity, build a better plan, and develop confidence in their own resources for overcoming difficulty?

Kohn and others argue that if we really want to help our children feel good about themselves, we should always treat them with respect, rather than shower them with praise. After all, what does the word "esteem" mean? It is a synonym for "respect." Self-esteem is, therefore, largely a product or reflection of self-respect.

Just as we teach responsibility by giving children responsibilities, we teach self-respect by giving our children respect. When children are treated with respect and are affirmed for their efforts to face challenges and to show respect for others, the result is healthy self-esteem.

XI

The Seven Essential Virtues of Moral Intelligence

by Michele Borba

Moral intelligence consists of seven essential *virtues — empathy, conscience, self-control, respect, kindness, tolerance,* and *fairness* — that help your child navigate through the ethical challenges and pressures she will inevitably face throughout life. These core virtues are what give her the moral bearings by which to stay on the path of goodness and to help her behave morally. Or, as a seven-year-old told me, "They're the things in me that help me be good." *And all can be taught, modeled, inspired, and reinforced so that your child can achieve them.* Here are the seven essential virtues that will nurture a lifelong sense of decency in your child:

1. *Empathy* is the core moral emotion that allows your child to understand how other people feel. This is the virtue that helps him become more sensitive to the needs and feelings of others, be more likely to help those who are hurt or troubled, and treat others more compassionately. It is also the powerful moral emotion that urges your child to do what is right because he can recognize the impact of emotional pain on others, stopping him from acting cruelly.

2. *Conscience* is a strong inner voice that helps your child decide right from wrong and stay on the moral path, zapping her with a dose of guilt whenever she strays. This virtue fortifies your child against forces countering goodness and

enables her to act right even in the face of temptation. It is the cornerstone for the development of the crucial virtues of honesty, responsibility, and integrity.

3. *Self-control* helps your child restrain his impulses and think before he acts so that he behaves right and is less likely to make rash choices with potentially dangerous outcomes. This is the virtue that helps your child become self-reliant because he knows he can control his actions. It is also the virtue that motivates generosity and kindness because it helps your child put aside what would give him immediate gratification and stirs his conscience to do something for someone else instead.

4. *Respect* encourages your child to treat others with consideration because she regards them as worthy. This is the virtue that leads your child to treat others the way she would like to be treated, and so lays the foundation to preventing violence, injustice, and hatred. When your child makes respect a part of her daily living, she will be more likely to care about the rights and feelings of others; as a result, she will show greater respect for herself, too.

5 *Kindness* helps your child show his concern about the welfare and feelings of others. By developing this virtue, your child will become less selfish and more compassionate, and he will understand that treating others kindly is simply the right thing to do. When your child achieves kindness, he will think more about the needs of others, show concern, offer to help those in need, and stick up for those who are hurt or troubled.

6. *Tolerance* helps your child appreciate different qualities in others, stay open to new perspectives and beliefs, and respect others regardless of differences in race, gender, appearance, culture, beliefs, abilities, or sexual orientation. This is the virtue that influences your child to treat others with kindness and understanding, to stand up against hatred, violence, and bigotry, and to respect people primarily on the basis of their character.

7. *Fairness* leads your child to treat others in a righteous, impartial, and just way so that she will be more likely to play by the rules, take turns and share, and listen openly to all sides before judging. Because this virtue increases your child's moral sensitivity, she will have the courage to stick up for those treated unfairly and demand that all people — regardless of race, culture, economic status, ability, or creed — be regarded equally.

MORAL INTELLIGENCE BUILDER
The Seven Essential Virtues of
Moral Intelligence and Solid Character

The seven essential virtues that follow comprise the complete plan for building your child's moral intelligence provided in this book [The author's *Building Moral Intelligence*]. These seven traits are what your child needs most to do what's right and resist any pressures that may defy the habits of solid character and good ethical living.

Virtue	*Definition*
Empathy	Identifying with and feeling other people's concerns
Conscience	Knowing the right and decent way to act and acting that way
Self-control	Regulating your thoughts and actions so that you stop any pressures from within or without and act the way you know and feel is right
Respect	Showing you value others by treating them in a courteous and considerate way
Kindness	Demonstrating concern about the welfare and feelings of others
Tolerance	Respecting the dignity and rights of all persons, even those whose beliefs and behaviors differ from your own
Fairness	Choosing to be open-minded and to act in a just and fair way

XII

Native American Education

by Joseph Bruchac

In large part, Western education today tends to be didactic. From books, lectures, filmstrips, and movies, we learn *about* things but rarely actually do them. We then test the knowledge, which has been gained by having our students answer questions *about* the things they have "learned." There are, of course, good reasons for this. The world, which our children must learn about, is too broad for them to have a hands-on approach to everything. However, as many educators have observed, too often the result of such education is rote learning that is more of a conditioned reflex than a true understanding. Further, the artificial divisions between fields of knowledge — with natural science, alone, divided into botany, zoology, geology, astronomy and literally hundreds of other subdivisions and areas of study — can produce a situation in which your result is the kind of knowledge one gains in dissecting a frog. You know its parts, but you cannot put them together. And, in cutting it apart, you have killed that frog.

Native American education, on the other hand, has always tended to be experiential and holistic. People learn by doing things. If one wishes to learn how to make baskets, one goes to a person making baskets and watches them as they work. If you are patient and watch long enough, eventually that basket maker may ask you to do something, to hold onto this coil of sweetgrass here, to help shave down this strip of ash. Eventually, over a period of time, you discover that you, too, know how to make a basket. But making a basket is not all that you have learned. A basket maker has to know which trees and other plants can be used and at which times of year they can be prepared. Thus, a knowledge of botany and of the rhythms of the seasons is required. When cutting a tree or uprooting a clump of sweetgrass, a basket maker must give thanks to that plant for sacrificing its life to help human beings survive. Tobacco is left in exchange for that sacrifice. Thus, there is a religious component to basket making. There are stories, also, to be learned about the baskets, about the items used in their crafting, about the significance of patterns and designs that are a part of the basket. Among the Pima people, the figures of the whirlwind or the man in the maze appear on baskets and have stories connected to them, which must be learned. There may even be songs.

A Pomo woman basket maker once sang her basket song for me as she worked, explaining that it must be done a certain number of times in just such a way when making a basket. When the song ended, the basket was done. Thus, making a basket is not something to be easily learned out of a book. For American Indian basket makers (and, I am sure, basket makers in other traditional cultures), it involves much more than just simple handcraft.

Children, as any sensible teacher knows, respond to doing things. Activities are almost always the favorite part of a day for a child in school. Imagine, then, a school made up of nothing but activities, and you may be able to better understand why this method of teaching was so widely practiced among Native American people. Children also respond to stories. A good story, in fact, is very much like doing something, for it takes the listener along and involves that listener in such a way that the events of the story come alive and the trials and accomplishments of the central character become those of the listener, who is more of a participant than a passive observer (as is the case with television). ...

JOSEPH BRUCHAC

Storytelling

When Tehanetorens [Ray Fadden is an elder whose Mohawk name is Tehanetorens. He is the founder of the Six Nations Indian Museum in Onchiota, New York] first taught in Indian schools in New York State, the idea of imbuing children with traditional Iroquois values or even using Indian storytelling as a part of a school curriculum was unthought of or forbidden. Western concepts of education have been so foreign to American Indian students — with the emphasis placed on didacticism and the Western tendency to depersonalize the universe — that it is no surprise that schools have been a hostile environment for all too many American Indians. Today, thanks to work such as his, something closer to the old patterns of Indian teaching may be found within the walls of such institutions as the Onondaga Nation School in Nedrow, New York, in the heart of the Onondaga Reservation. A school run by the Onondaga community with the approval of the state education department, ONS makes use of old patterns in very special ways. Their Indian heritage is even honored by the school calendar, which provides a vacation for students and staff during the time of the Midwinter Ceremonials that come each year when the Dancing Stars — which Europeans call the "Pleiades" — are at the very height of the winter sky. During the time of the traditional Thanksgiving to the Maple Trees, when the sap is gathered in March, there is a maple festival at the school, and a sugarhouse is kept running out back, close to the school kitchen, cooking down the sap from trees tapped by the students. When it is the time to dig wild onions, a group of students and teachers gather during the day to go out into the fields around the school and harvest.

In the bilingual classroom, supervised by Audrey Shenandoah, storytelling is one of the favorite activities in the room, and students from the preschoolers to those in the upper grades take part. The Onondaga students introduce themselves to a visitor by speaking their clan names and their Indian names in Onondaga. The walls and pillars of the basement room are decorated with paintings of animals and figures from Iroquois mythology. Looking at those pictures, of Wolf and Eel, Snipe and Bear and Deer, one sees that such Native American traditions as that of the "clan animals" create a sense of closeness to nature from birth, which most young people of European ancestry have never experienced.

Among the Iroquois (and most other Native American peoples throughout the continent), you are born into a clan. In the case of the Iroquois, you inherit your clan from your mother. Each clan is represented by an animal (among some other native peoples, such natural forces as Sky or Wind, may take the place of a clan animal), and you feel a particular closeness to it. Just as the majority culture's ideas of astrology (enormously popular ideas, as often as they are debunked or scoffed at) indicate that you are affected by your star sign, so too, one's clan seems to have some effect on one's personality. I have often heard it said that members of the Bear Clan tend to be big, strong people, that those who are "Wolves" are quick moving and volatile, that "Turtles" are slow moving and careful. Certain traditional stories are associated with different clans. There is a Mohawk story, for example, of how the Bear Clan was given the secrets of medicine plants by the Creator. Throughout the continent there are "bear doctors," and it is said that bears suffer from many of the same sicknesses people do and that by watching what herbs a bear eats when it is sick, one may learn to cure certain human illnesses.

Having a clan animal with which one is intimately connected is only one way in which American Indian culture and stories create a sense of closeness to nature for Native children. The forces of nature are personified in ways that I feel to be essentially nonromantic and usefully realistic. The four winds, for example, are associated with certain animals. The north wind is called the "White Bear" by certain American Indian nations. It is strong and cold and brings the snow. The east wind is called the "Moose" by the people of the northern Maritimes. They see it walking out of the water with its great strength and shaking the moisture from its wide antlers. The south wind is the gentle "Fawn." When it arrives it comes with the warmth, the new flowers, the green grass. The west wind is the "Panther," striking with sudden force. Such names accurately describe the characteristics of these winds, are easy to remember and also make the forces of nature — because they are better understood in the shapes of animals — less threatening.

Even the calendar is seen differently through the eyes of American Indian culture and stories. Instead of learning the names of the months of the year through the old rhyme "thirty days has September, ..." American Indian children are still, through their elders and in schools such as ONS, taught the thirteen moons. Each moon is named according to some event taking place in nature at that time of year. For the Abenaki, the time around November is *Mzatonos,* the "Moon of Freezing"; the time around October is *Pebonkas,* the "Moon of Leaves Falling"; and around May is *Kikas,* "Planting Moon." Each Native people has its own names for the moon cycles, names which reflect the condition of the natural world and also remind the human beings of the activities they should be undertaking.

XIII

The Twenty-Four Gurus

by Swami Sivananda

In the *Śrīmad Bhāgavatam* there is a profound but simple teaching given to King Yadu by Dattatreya, a wandering renunciate (*avadhūt)*), who is asked by the King to explain the reason for his spiritual effulgence. This masterful response of the illustrious hermit comes forth as the *Avadhūta Gītā* and demonstrates how profound learning can come from the most unsuspecting sources. King Yadu, who, on seeing Dattatreya so happy, asked him the secret of his happiness and the name of his Guru. Dattatreya said, "The Self alone is my Guru. Yet, I have learned wisdom from twenty-four other individuals and objects. So they, too, are also my Gurus." Dattatreya then mentioned the names of his twenty-four Gurus and spoke of the wisdom that he had learned from each as follows:

"The names of my twenty-four Gurus are earth, water, fire, sky, moon, sun, pigeon, python, ocean, moth, honey-gatherers (black bee), bees, elephant, deer, fish, the dancing-girl Pingala, raven, child, maiden, serpent, arrow-maker, spider and beetle.

1. I learned patience and doing good to others from the *earth*.
2. From *water,* I learned the quality of purity.
3. I learned from *air* to be without attachment though I move with many people in this world.
4. From *fire* I learned to glow with the splendor of Self-knowledge and austerity.

5. I learned from the *sky* that the Self is all-pervading and yet it has no contact with any object.

6. I learned from the *moon* that the Self is always perfect and changeless and it is only the limiting adjuncts that cast shadows over it.

7. Just as a sun reflected in various pots of water appears as so many different reflections, so also *Brahman* appears different because of the bodies caused by the reflection through the mind. This is the lesson I have learned from the *sun*.

8. I once saw a pair of *pigeons* with their young birds. A fowler spread a net and caught the young birds. The mother pigeon was very much attached to her children. She fell into the net and was caught. From this I have learned that attachment is the root cause of earthly bondage.

9. The *python* does not move about for its food. It remains contented with whatever it gets, lying in one place. From this I learned to be unmindful of food and to be contented with whatever I get to eat.

10. Just as the *ocean* remains unmoved, even though hundreds of rivers flow into it, so also the wise man should remain unmoved among all the various sorts of temptations, difficulties and troubles.

11. To control the sense of sight and to fix the mind on the Self, is the lesson I learned from the *moth*.

12. I take a little food from one house and a little from another house and thus appease my hunger. I am not a burden on the householder. This I learned from the *black bee* which gathers honey from various flowers.

13. *Bees* collect honey with great trouble, but a hunter comes along and takes the honey away easily. From this I learned that it is useless to hoard things.

14. The male *elephant,* blinded by lust, falls into a pit covered with grass, even at the sight of a female elephant. Therefore, one should destroy lust.

15. The *deer* is enticed and trapped by the hunter through its love of music. Therefore, one should never listen to lewd songs.

16. Just as a *fish* that is covetous of food falls an easy victim to the bait, so also the man who is greedy for food loses his independence and easily gets ruined.

17. There was a *dancing girl* named Pingala. Being tired of looking for customers, one night she became hopeless. She had to be contented with what traffic she had that day and retired to a sound sleep. I learned from this fallen woman the lesson that the abandonment of hopelessness leads to contentment.

18. A *raven* picked up a piece of flesh. It was pursued and beaten by other birds. It dropped the piece of flesh and attained peace and rest. From this I learned that a man in the world undergoes all sorts of troubles and miseries when he runs after sensual pleasures and that he becomes as happy as the bird when he abandons them.

19. The *child* who sucks milk is free from all cares, worries, and anxieties, and is always cheerful. I learned the virtue of cheerfulness from the child.

20. The *maiden* was husking paddy. Her bangles made much noise and there were visitors from her husband's house. To silence the bangles, she removed them, one by one. Even when there were just two, they produced some noise. When she had only one, it did not make any noise, and she was happy. I learned from the maiden that living among many would create discord, disturbance, dispute, and quarrel. Even among two there might be unnecessary words or strife. The ascetic or the *saṁnyāsin* should remain alone in solitude.

21. A *serpent* does not build its own hole. It dwells in the holes dug out by others. Even so, an ascetic should not build a home for himself. He should live in a temple or a cave built by others.

22. I learned from the *arrow-maker* the quality of intense concentration of mind.

23. The *spider* pours out of its mouth long threads and weaves them into cobwebs. Then it gets itself entangled in the net of its own making. Even so, man makes a net of his own ideas

and gets entangled in it. The wise man should, therefore, abandon all worldly thoughts and think of *Brahman* only.

24. The *beetle* catches hold of a worm, puts it in its nest and gives it a sting. The poor worm, always fearing the return of the beetle and sting, and thinking constantly of the beetle, becomes a beetle itself. I learned from the beetle and the worm to turn myself into the Self by contemplating constantly on It; thus I gave up all attachment to the body and attained liberation."

The king was highly impressed by listening to these enlightening words of Lord Dattatreya. He abandoned the world and practiced constant meditation on the Self. Dattatreya was absolutely free from intolerance or prejudice of any kind and learned wisdom from whatever source it came.

XIV

On the Road to Find Out

by Rafe Esquith

After nine years in the classroom filled with many successes and just as many mistakes, I was still standing. The Musketeers [three students who had given the author a hard time] had really injured me, and I was in a bad place. Yes, I knew that the most important thing in teaching and parenting (and life) is to know who you are. I just hadn't found the answer. And let me make it clear that the answer for me is certainly not going to be the right answer for you. I just knew that I could never be a good teacher without defining myself — a sort of personal mission statement.

I thought I was there. In my first few years of teaching, the one thing I could count on was teaching literature to children. As previously mentioned, I taught books that meant something to me, and I began to love one book more than the others. In doing so, I began to relate to one character more than any other. For several years this book and character became the highlight of my year of reading great novels with the students. It was Mark Twain's masterpiece, *The Adventures of Huckleberry Finn*.

God, did I love Huck. I still do. He is such a good person. He constantly makes the sound moral choice even though he believes himself to be evil. I loved Twain's brilliant use of irony. Most of all, I loved Jim and Huck's journey down the river. Two lost souls on the highway of life, to quote *Damn Yankees*. And most of all, I loved the end of the book.

In case you've forgotten, Huck and Jim both run away from society. It's a society filled with violence and racism and hypocrisy and dishonesty and meanness. Yet these two outcasts use their wits and love for each other to escape one predicament after another. And at the end of this long journey, Huck is given a chance to return to civilization. He has a chance to be raised "properly" and do things the way society wants him to.

And Huck, God bless him, rejects society. He's been there before. He decides to take Jim and Tom Sawyer and light out for the territory. Good for you, Huck! You tell them! Tell all those awful people off.

I believed that Huck had replaced Roy Hobbs as my role model. I, too, would reject society, and a school system damaged beyond repair. If a few cool kids wanted to light out for the territory with me, they were welcome to come aboard the raft on which I sailed.

Except, I had come to a point where no one was getting on board the raft with me. I loved Huck, but I was still lost. I thought I knew who I was, but to be Huck was not to be a great teacher.

It took a ten-year-old to challenge and humble me into seeing that Huck was not the answer for me. It was the first day of my new class. The Musketeers were gone but my nerves were exposed and raw. I was in no mood to be a good teacher. I just knew that no kid was ever going to use and abuse me the way those three ingrates had. It was easier being mad at them than being mad at myself.

As my students entered the first day, a tiny little girl with bangs came up to me. In a bag she had some breakfast food purchased at a fast-food store, and she told me she had bought me breakfast for our first day together.

"What's your name?" I asked her.

"Joann," she said quietly.

"Well, listen then, Joann," I said. "You don't have to buy me breakfast or kiss up to me. If you want to be successful in this class, just do your best and we'll get along just fine — but no presents — got it?"

Yes," she said and found a seat.

The first week went by smoothly. On Friday, I gathered the students in what we call a Magic Circle. The students sit in a circle and share their feelings about any and all issues, ranging from school subjects to family problems.

"Well," I told them proudly, "I think we've had a good first week. Our reading and math have been excellent, and everyone is doing a fine job. Does anyone have anything to say about this week we've spent together?"

For the first time since Monday, Joann raised her hand. "I have something to say, Rafe," she began. "You know, last Monday, when I brought you breakfast, I wasn't trying to kiss up to you. You really don't understand." She went on softly but with the determination and confidence of someone speaking the truth from the heart. "I've been waiting my whole life to be in your class. Ever since I was a first-grader, I've watched your class. You always have the coolest things. You have the best kids. You have great plays and play the best music. Your kids have the most fun. My parents think you're a god. They've seen you on television and read about you in newspapers and magazines."

Man, the room was quiet. This little girl was on a roll.

"I wasn't trying to kiss up to you. I was just so happy to be here that I wanted to tell you that. I wanted to tell you how happy I was that I was going to have you for my teacher. And you really hurt my feelings. I wanted you to know that you really hurt me."

I was devastated. This little girl spoke so simply and honestly that there was only one thing I could do. To borrow from Holden Caulfield, I apologized like a madman. I promised her that if she ever gave me another chance, I would never treat her like that again.

Finding My Hero

Battered and bruised but not defeated, I began work with this new class. One night, as I've said, my wife suggested to me that it was time to reread a particular book. It was a book I had read twice before and loved both times. Yet I hadn't really understood it. I was now ready to find the role model who had the answer for me. I reread Harper Lee's *To Kill a Mockingbird*, and I realized I had found my hero in Atticus Finch.

I had thought this novel was about a trial. It is, of course, but it's about much more than that. Early in the story, Atticus returns home to find his little daughter, Scout, crying. She has been brutally teased at school and asks her father, "Atticus, do you defend niggers?"

When Atticus corrects her racist remark, Scout merely explains that it's not her word but what the children are saying at school. She can't understand why Atticus is defending someone when the whole town doesn't think he should. Why is he doing this?

"For a number of reasons," Atticus replies. The most important one, he explains, is that if he didn't, he could never tell his children what to do anymore. He could not hold his head up in front of them.

Atticus's son, Jem, asks his father if they're going to win the case, and Atticus replies quietly, "No."

It hit me like a thunderbolt. You see, Atticus knows everything Huck knows. He knows society is racist. He recognizes the violence, hypocrisy, injustice, and ignorance of society. He knows he is going to lose.

But Atticus does not light out for the territory. He goes into the courtroom to fight the fight as best as he can, because it is what he believes in. He doesn't do it because of the law, or the rules, or what people will think. He has his own code, and he lives by it as well as he can.

I still cry when I think about this. My classroom is my courtroom. I am going to lose more than I win. There are many times when, despite my efforts, I will lose children to poverty, ignorance, and, most tragically, a society that embraces mediocrity.

But that doesn't paralyze me anymore. I have a code, as any good teacher or parent must have. It doesn't matter if I lost a battle yesterday. It doesn't matter if the odds are against me. It doesn't matter if I'm just one fellow trying to fight television, corporations, and a society that hasn't yet achieved Dr. Martin Luther King's dream of judging someone by the content of his character.

I knew that I had to be the person I wanted the kids to be. I never want my kids to be depressed or despairing about any bad breaks or failures that they've had. Well, that had to apply to me as well. I now knew that if I wanted the kids to work hard, then I'd better be the hardest-working person they'd ever known. If I wanted them to be kind, I'd better be the kindest human being they'd ever met. Teaching must be by example, not by lecture.

I've made plenty of mistakes since rediscovering Atticus, but I've always been able to hold my head up to my students. Atticus showed me the way.

PART THREE

Teachers and Schools

The mediocre teacher tells
The good teacher explains
The superior teacher demonstrates
The great teacher inspires

William Arthur Ward

Critics of today's schools often complain that the schools have lost their "academic purpose." However, it is that academic purpose, pursued relentlessly and sometimes cruelly, that drove large numbers of young people out of the schools in an earlier, "more rigorous" era. One purpose of schooling should be to develop the intellect, but that does not mean to stuff the heads of children with material arbitrarily chosen by experts and designed to rank and sort them.

It means rather to guide students toward the intelligent use of their intellectual capacities in both personal and public life. It means equipping them with the power to evaluate and direct change, to resist harmful changes and promote those that contribute to human flourishing. Almost any subject matter of genuine interest to students, well taught, can contribute to this end.

Nel Noddings
Happiness and Education

XV

Our Children
by Swami Chinmayananda

[The following article is based on a paper sent by Swami Chinmayananda to the First National Conference of principals, headmasters, and correspondents of Chinmaya Vidyalayas, held at Bangalore in May 1985.]

The child is not a miniature adult. Therefore we should not try to cram into him our adult ideas in his early years. He has his own way of seeing and enjoying things and responding to day-to-day happenings. Let him live his life and grow up to appreciate his poetic world of ideals, rather than drive him to learn the more practical rules of life.

It is Rousseau who insisted upon the importance of a healthy environment at home for a child and who stressed the importance of the influence of the mother upon the growing child. He pleaded for the child's rights. His writings called for a redefinition of parental responsibilities. They made such an important impact on the existing values and beliefs that the French Parliament condemned the book and ordered every printed copy to be confiscated and burnt!

Rousseau's ideas were a reaction to the breakup of family life in the Europe of his times. It was a plea to women, as mothers, not to neglect their responsibilities towards their offspring. No "nannies" can replace a mother. He stated "where there is no mother, there is no child." He insisted upon liberty, freedom of movement and free-play of all the five senses of the child. Do not rush the child into premature speech, he wrote. When he has something to say he will discover the words to express it. Leave him alone.

To Rousseau, the object of education is not vocational: it is to produce a man out of the child. "A well-educated man is he who is best equipped to bear the fortunes and misfortunes of life," declared Rousseau very eloquently, as though echoing the ideas of the Rishis, which we find in our ancient treatises on education.

Leo Tolstoy had his own theories on education and these were much influenced by Rousseau's ideas. He opened a school for the simple peasant children where there was no punishment meted out for being late or absent: "If the school is run properly, children will run to their class well or ill," was his argument. The main thrust of early education in his school was on reading out stories and fables, from the Bible and from literature. When the children got interested they taught themselves to read with minimum help!

Homer Lane is yet another daring educationist who conducted experiments in the countryside outside London. He viewed children who committed crimes from a distinctive angle. Instead of pitying them as "poor little sinners," he admired their vigorous dynamism and considered them as stouthearted little ruffians. For him they all had admirable qualities but these were misapplied. He sought to channelize their over-enthusiasm and give a purposeful direction to their sense of heroism. For him, that was true education as it helped retrieve children from their wrong ways, enabling them to become successful men.

Lane believed in the efficacy of work to discipline the minds of children — not just work thrust upon them but work that they voluntarily took up and enjoyed doing. Rudolf Steiner, Maria Montessori and Rabindranath Tagore are others who gave much thought to systems of educating growing children.

Self-Education

We all start our career at birth arriving into a strange world with no evident knowledge of it. Thereafter starts our struggle to experiment and discover our abilities to see, hear, smell, taste, and touch. After that we learn how to move, coordinate, and function with our main instruments of action. When the child has crawled out of his infancy and reached the stage when he can move about, watch and observe, he is fit for self-education. The child's endless sense of wonder at things, his steady sense of inquisitiveness, his silent but very thoughtful attention to everything said and done around him in his world, his experiments with love, affection, anger, jealousy, covetousness, instinct of acquisition, grabbing, fighting, kindness — the entire gamut of emotional life — is the next stage. During this time education starts and this highly impressive period is the most crucial time in building up the child's entire future.

At this juncture, his main study is from example and he imitates all the elders that he watches around him: parents, servants, maids, neighbors, their children, and visitors. From everyone children pick up certain traits, habits, words, ideas, dress sense, even their accent and inflections of speech. The child is never tired of observing and learning from everyone and from every situation.

Hence it is important to provide the child, at this nursery level, with a happy and cheerful atmosphere; and with the ideals of affection, tenderness, concern for other living beings, appreciation of the good and the noble, recognition of beauty in things, and charm in people. Children are slow to grasp the subtle; therefore, we have to openly exaggerate the noble virtues — be a bit shamelessly demonstrative. Touch the children. Tell them that you love them, that they are beautiful, intelligent, good, and noble. Repeat that again and again! Demonstrate your readiness to sacrifice for others. Let children see that you are very anxious to be helpful to others. This can very quickly impress them and sink into their personality. Thus noble character is easily formed.

The teacher is a twenty-four hours, 365-days-a-year professional. Children are very observant, especially of their teachers for whom they have love and respect. No action of the teacher is insignificant to the children. They watch and watch, and learn to imitate and reflect upon their teacher's actions and words.

When the child is five, he becomes fit for regular schooling. Everywhere the entrance to primary classes starts at five. Now his limbs are steady. A healthy child has enormous energy to burn up and needs frequent refreshment to replenish the energy drained away in playing, fighting, running around and also in studying, singing, howling, and screaming.

Now we must start taming his behavior to enable him to conform to a happy social life with others, while he is encouraged to grow in his knowledge and abilities. Art and craft classes provide the best environment in which to polish behavior. The wild ones are to be especially treated with love and kind persuasion. In extreme cases punishment must be given in the presence of all other children, as an example. Yet, never show any rancor towards the punished child. Keep on loving him, and express your endless concern for his safety and comfort.

Emphasizing Values

From five to ten, the child stretches his emotional and intellectual abilities into ever-widening fields and this is the right time to emphasize the higher and noble values of life. This is done through stories, and children pick up their own ideals to admire and revere. The Puranic stories, toned down to their level of understanding, stories of great saints and sages, mighty heroes of science and politics and social workers who had molded the character of people, are all very easily absorbed by them. Animal stories from the *Pañcataṅtra* hammer into them the concepts of good and their distinctive features. They will see how in the confrontation of good and evil, the good alone wins in the end. Recitations, mass chantings, and group songs are very effective at this stage.

Between the ages of ten and fourteen, they need a little more material to handle as their minds have unfolded to a greater extent. Now the child appreciates ideas that it can wrestle with and enjoys the flashes of wonder at understanding life and its ways. At this stage they can enjoy and enrich their minds with books like *Gītā for Children*.

For individuals in the age group of fifteen to eighteen years, help them to sink their ideas into their own minds. Encourage them to express their opinions on things they have studied. They must be helped to overcome their shyness. Encourage them through compliments and generous presents for what they have tried to express. Never, at this stage, should we criticize the mistakes they make. Leave them alone to grow up — do not hasten them.

When they are between eighteen and twenty years, they have reached a fuller stage of mental and physical development. Now they are ready to have a deeper understanding and this is the time to introduce them to the early steps in *sādhanā* (spiritual practice). This will enable them, when they are by themselves, to discover that with diligence and practice, they can control the mad onrush of their own wild and crazy mind. A little *japa* and daily sessions of a few moments of inner quietude of the mind will be very helpful to them. We can slowly lift them to a conviction in themselves that "man needs self-control if he is to control his own mind." Without such a tuned-in mind, excellence in life's activities cannot be assured.

When the youngster reaches perhaps twenty or twenty-five, he is ready to be initiated into the highest. Without any hesitation teach him or her the Upanishads (*Īśa*, *Kena*, and *Kaṭha*) and the *Bhagavad Gītā* (Chapters II, III, VI, IX, XII, and XIII). The rest he can study by himself. Leave him alone to grow up at his own pace.

This kind of a graded system, if followed faithfully, will enable us to complete the education of our growing generation more effectively, both in their inner values of life and also in the outer objective sciences. The secular education will make them proficient to meet the challenges in their professions, and the values of life inculcated will mold them to be better persons in society.

Can we conceive and plan out in every detail a system of education for our children based upon the above ideas? This will be the job of our educationists. Will they take up this national challenge and face it wisely with determination and courage?

XVI

Tagore: Education for Spiritual Fulfillment

by *Takuya Kaneda*

Tagore defined the object of education as to give the unity of truth and said:

> Formerly when life was simple all the different elements of man were in complete harmony. But when there came the separation of the intellect from the spiritual and physical, school education put its entire emphasis on the intellect and the physical side of man. We devote our sole attention to giving children information, not knowing that by this emphasis we are accentuating a break between the intellectual, physical, and the spiritual life. (Tagore, R., *Personality*, 1917, p. 126)

Tagore's idea of education developed from the tradition of Hinduism, but his idea was not limited to the narrow meaning of Hinduism. He had been to Europe and the United States several times and deeply understood Western culture as well as his own. He attempted to pursue universal truth beyond the differences between East and West. Hinduism is likely to imply exclusive religious customs in a particular region yet the original philosophy of Hinduism was actually quite universal. The name, Hindu, was derived from a term used by outsiders to imply the place where people maintained the special spiritual beliefs and practices based on the Vedas and the Upanishads, the sacred ancient literature of India. The indigenous inhabitants did not have any consciousness that they themselves were exclusively Hindus. They thought that the fundamental idea of their religion was universal although they practiced their own religious customs. In this idea of universal religion, all religions were the same in their spiritual pursuit for the truth beyond differences in religious customs, which were as various as languages and which also differed from place to place. The solidification of the concept of Hinduism was developed as part of a reaction to encroaching Islam and a result of the emergence of nationalism during British colonialism. Tagore, however, followed Hinduism's original philosophy of a universal religion, the essence of the Upanishads; he applied it to his school by emphasizing the essential role of spiritual growth in education.

Tagore simply mentioned spirituality as follows:

> I believe in a spiritual world — not as anything separate from this world — but as its innermost truth. With the breath we draw we must always feel this truth, that we are living in God. Born in this great world, full of the mystery of the infinite, we cannot accept our existence as a momentary outburst of chance, drifting on the current matter towards an eternal nowhere. (Tagore, R., *Personality*, 1917)

He claimed that spiritual reality was missed "by our incessant habit of ignoring it from childhood". To fulfill spiritual growth in education, Tagore proposed an entirely different picture of school from ordinary modern schools. This idea stemmed from an educational custom in ancient India.

Ancient Idea of Learning

There was an idea of four different stages of life in ancient India. The first stage is called *Brahmacarya*, the period of discipline and education. *Gṛhastha* is the second period of life, in which one has a spouse and raises children to fulfill family and social life. *Vānaprastha* is the third period of life when one concentrates on spiritual life in the forest after fulfillment of family and social duties. *Saṁnyāsa* is the last period of life. In this period, it is necessary to abandon material necessities, to lead an austere life, and to seek a spiritual path. The first stage of *Brahmacarya* was very important to establish the physical, mental, and spiritual base on which the following phases of life could be solidly built.

Tagore regarded this *Brahmacarya* as an ideal form of education for young students. When he reached forty in 1901, he started his ideal education center at a remote and peaceful place, Shantiniketan, in Bolpur of Bengal. This beautiful, natural setting had been previously chosen by the poet's father, Devendranath, as a retreat for spiritual pursuit. He had named it Shantiniketan, "the abode of peace." The school was literally an "*āśrama*" at the stage of *Brahmacarya*, that point of life in which it was essential for young students to live with a master in the forest. Living in the forest gave students the opportunity to encounter experiences, which could hardly be found in ordinary daily life. Tagore explained the relationship between "forest" and the ancient people in India, as follows:

> The forest entered into a close living relationship with their work and leisure, with their daily necessities and contemplations. They could not think of other surroundings as separate or inimical. So the view of truth, which these men found, did not make manifest the difference, but rather the unity of all things. They uttered their faith in these words: "*Yadidaṁ kiñca sarvaṁ prāṇa ejati niḥsṛtam*" (All that *is* vibrates with life, having come out from life). (Tagore, R., *Creative Unity*, 1922, pp. 47-48)

Tagore tried to make students isolated from the busy city life for their spiritual growth. He explained the reason: "The four elements of earth, water, air, and fire form a whole and are instinct with the universal soul — this knowledge cannot be gained at a school in town. A school in town is a factory which can only teach us to regard the world as a machine" (1961, *Towards Universal Man*, p. 73). He repeatedly emphasized the importance of simple living:

This we can attain during our childhood by daily living in a place where the truth of the spiritual world is not obscured by a crowd of necessities assuming artificial importance; where life is simple, surrounded by fullness of leisure, by ample space and pure air and profound peace of nature; and where men live with a perfect faith in the eternal life before them. (Tagore, R., *Personality*, 1917, p. 135)

Such a simple life was an essential part of the stage of *Brahmacarya*, when the teachers and their students had to live together as family members. Tagore mentioned that book-learning had not been regarded as the most important part of education in ancient India and pointed out that this idea could be sometimes found in the present traditional schools of orthodox Hindu learning. He explained: "They are surrounded by an atmosphere of culture, and the teachers are dedicated to their vocation. They live a simple life, without any material interest or luxury to distract their minds, and with plenty of time and opportunity for absorbing into their nature the things they learn." (Tagore, R., *Towards Universal Man*, 1961, p. 70)

XVII

The Educational Vision of Maria Montessori

by Ron Miller

> We must take into consideration that from birth the child has
> a power in him. We must not just see the child, but God in
> him. We must respect the laws of creation in him.
>
> *Maria Montessori[1]*

Maria Montessori pursued her educational work with a spiritual consciousness verging on mysticism. Although her ideas
have been packaged and practiced for ninety years as a "method" replete with cleverly designed materials and recognizable
classroom routines, Montessori's educational vision is far more
profound than this, and essentially aim for a complete transformation of virtually all modern assumption about teaching,
learning, childhood, and the very purpose of human existence
on this Earth. This was recognized as early as 1912 by one of
the first Americans to visit Montessori's experiment in Rome,
Dorothy Carfield Fisher, who reported that Montessori considered her "ideas, hope and visions" to be "much more essential"
than the techniques she had developed. Fisher continued,

> Contact with the new ideas is not doing for us what it ought,
> it does not act as a powerful stimulant to the whole body of
> our thought about life. It should make us think, and think
> hard not only about how to teach our children the alphabet
> more easily, but about such fundamental matters as what we

actually mean by moral life; whether we really honestly wish the spiritually best for our children, or only the materially best; why we are really in the world at all. In many ways, this "Montessori System" is a new religion which we are called upon to help bring into the world, and we cannot aid in so great an undertaking without considerable spiritual as well as intellectual travail.[2]

Much more recently, Aline Wolf, a Montessori educator for nearly forty years, reaffirmed this position, arguing that it was time for her colleagues to make the spiritual vision at the heart of Montessori's work far more visible and explicit.[3] This shall be the intent of my essay. ...

A Holistic Vision of the Universe

The blend of science and religion in Montessori's worldview forms the basis for a truly *holistic* conception of the universe. Similarly to fellow Catholic theologian/scientists Teilhard de Chardin and Thomas Berry (among others), and in a way not unlike the "spiritual science" of Rudolf Steiner, Montessori looked carefully and deeply into the world of nature and found, not isolated material entities interacting mechanically, but a living and purposeful Cosmos. "All things are part of the universe, and are connected with each other to form one whole unity".[4] She was deeply impressed by the *harmony* she discerned in the natural world, the ecology of existence that gives every living thing a meaningful function in the larger system. Every species, indeed every individual organism, contributes to the good of the whole by performing its inherent "cosmic" function. This harmony has not emerged randomly, but expresses "a pre-established plan" that is "of divine origin;" she was convinced that "the purpose of life is to obey the occult command which harmonizes all and creates an ever better world".[5] The Cosmos is engaged in a process of evolution toward ever-greater harmony — toward the fulfillment of God's mysterious purpose.

The guiding belief of Montessori's educational philosophy, the fundamental point around which all her principles and techniques revolve, is her conviction that *humanity has its own special function to fulfill in this divine evolution.* The human species is "God's prime agent in creation" and it is our responsibility to "learn to do more effectively our share of work in the cosmic plan".[6] Evolution is not yet complete; God's purpose has not yet been achieved, and the mission of human life is to give expression to the formative forces within us that are yearning to complete the cosmic plan. We are called to work in partnership with the divine. This understanding of our existence places all our endeavors — our cultural, political, economic, and even our most personal strivings — in an entirely spiritual light: "The world was not created for us to enjoy," Montessori proclaims, "but we are created in order to evolve the cosmos".[7] In an earlier essay,[8] I argued that this striking statement is consistent with the teachings of great moral sages such as Martin Luther King, Jr., Abraham Heschel, and Krishnamurti, who all similarly asserted that we are on this Earth to contribute to the unfolding of divine justice, harmony and wisdom, not merely to amuse ourselves or satisfy our many material and sensual desires. In this light, education is not to be seen merely as preparation for a successful career or any sort of social or intellectual distinction; rather, education is the process of awakening the divine formative forces within every person's soul that enable the individual to make his or her own unique contribution to the cosmic plan, to fulfill his or her own destiny.

Montessori wrote that humanity's role in evolution is to construct a "supra-nature" — a social, cultural and technological extension of nature that calls forth ever greater dimensions of human creativity and understanding — a notion very similar to Teilhard de Chardin's "noosphere." This is humanity's task because we, more than any other living species, "can receive the emanations of the Godhead" and transform divine plans into physical and cultural manifestations.[9] But she repeatedly observed that our material and technological progress had far outpaced our psychological, moral, and spiritual development, and in the twentieth century it was imperative that we make a determined effort toward remedying this imbalance. Modern societies, due to their pervasive materialism, have neglected the spiritual forces that animate the human being, and our institutions, particularly schooling, have become repressive and damaging, turning people into "slaves" of the machine rather than cultivating their spiritual sensitivity, she wrote. Modern people are ill prepared to deal with the great moral challenges of our age, and are unable to resist the demons of nationalism and war that threaten to engulf the world.

To address this imbalance, Montessori envisioned a curriculum for elementary school students that she called "cosmic education." The purpose of this approach is to provide the young person with an expansive, inspiring vision of the grandeur of the universe and one's personal destiny within it. This is an education that gives life meaning because all aspects of creation are shown to fit into a complex, interconnected whole that is far larger than our customary limited worldview. Aline D. Wolf comments that:

> The value of cosmic education, as I see it, is that it places the child's life in a spiritual perspective. No one can be confronted with the cosmic miracle and not see that there is more to life than our everyday experiences. Fast foods, designer sneakers, video games and sports heroes all pale beside the wonder of the universe.[10]

Cosmic education lifts the young person's consciousness out of the mundane, materialistic concerns of modern society and instills a sense of awe, touching a receptive and searching force within the soul.

This is exactly the sort of "spiritual reconstruction" that Montessori intended when she spoke at several international peace conferences in the 1930s, and asserted that only the spiritual renewal of humankind through education, not any superficial economic or political effort, could alter the violent course of human history: "The real danger threatening humanity is the emptiness in men's souls; all the rest is merely a consequence of this emptiness".[11] In recognition of her efforts, Montessori was nominated for the Nobel Peace Prize in 1949, 1950, and 1951.

Consistent with her holistic understanding, Montessori saw all of humanity as one nation, even one organism — an "organic unity." She considered people as fundamentally being citizens of the Cosmos beyond their social or cultural conditioning. Given technological developments of the modern age, she argued, it was time to put partial identities and false distinctions aside, and work together globally to achieve our "collective mission" of furthering the evolution of consciousness. It is education's task to encourage peaceful cooperation "and readiness to shed prejudices in the interests of common work for the cosmic plan, which may also be called the Will of God, actively expressed in the whole of His creation".[12] Her views on peace, social justice and democracy flowed from this holistic religious conviction that human beings all share the task of building a divinely ordered world. Idealism born of economic analysis or ideological conviction alone would not be sufficient. A socialist early in her life, at one point later in her career she addressed a group of communists and bluntly informed them that their social revolution would fail unless people were uplifted "towards the laws that govern human nature, which are connected to the very laws of the universe".[13] Democracy and justice *follow* from the unfolding of divine potentials, and social change is not authentic unless it springs from a genuine love of humanity, which is a spiritual, not simply an intellectual commitment.

FOOTNOTES:

[1] Maria Montessori (1989a). *The Child, Society and the World: Unpublished Speeches and Writings.* Compiled and edited by Günter Schulz-Benesch; translated by Caroline Juler and Heather Yesson.

[2] Fisher, Dorothy Canfield (1912). *A Montessori Mother.*

[3] Wolf, Aline D. (1996). *Nurturing the Spirit in Non-sectarian Classrooms.*

[4] Montessori, Maria (1948/1973). *To Educate the Human Potential,* p. 8.

5   Montessori, Maria (1946/1989b). *Education for a New World.*
6   Montessori, Maria (1948/1973). *To Educate the Human Potential,* p. 26, 33.
7   Montessori, Maria (1989b). *Education for a New World,* p. 22.
8   Miller, Ron (2000). "Education and the Evolution of the Cosmos" in *Caring for a New Life: Essays on Holistic Education.*
9   Montessori, Maria (1948/1972a). *Education and Peace.*
10 Wolf, Aline D. (1996). *Nurturing the Spirit in Non-sectarian Classrooms* p. 97.
11 Montessori, Maria (1949/1972a). *Education and Peace,* p. 44, 53.
12 Montessori, Maria (1948/1973). *To Educate the Human Potential,* p. 74.
13 Maria Montessori (1989a). *The Child, Society and the World: Unpublished Speeches and Writings.* Compiled and edited by Günter Schulz-Benesch; translated by Caroline Juler and Heather Yesson, p. 101.

XVIII

Education for a Deeper Sense of Self

by John Donnelly

Education, to me, is not theory. It is not requirements. It is not lesson plans. Education is felt. It is shared. It is a commitment to all the children of the earth and to all the flora and fauna of the planet. It is the realization that holistic learning, spiritual practices, and sacred space are not elements to shy away from or fear, but instead are the bonds that hold all of us together. Education includes the understanding that the search for a deeper sense of self is not a passive activity. We know that curing the ills of the world may not come overnight. It may not come in a generation, or even in a century or a millennium. But I believe it will come, and it starts with each one of us: one teacher providing understanding to one student; one practitioner creating a compassionate act; one facilitator creating the opportunity for engaged service. Simply put: it is making the world better, one step at a time. As Gill stated:

> As long as there is strife and human suffering in the global village, there will be a need for educational reform. As long as there is a need for human rights and for an informed society, there will be a need to consider morality and literacy. Until all the world's citizens can function effectively in their native lands and be their "brother's keeper," there will be a need for educational change. The highest reward for a man's toil is not what he gets for it, but what he becomes by it.[1]

There lives within each human spirit a sense of doing what is right. There is something that creates feelings of helpfulness, caring and giving. To this end every educator in every classroom throughout the world should strive to bring this sense of potential to each child they meet. As Purpel states:

> I believe that in order for individuals to be compassionate, they must be open to feel the inner impulse to feel connected to all people; people need to have a sense of freedom, agency, and hope. I further believe that those capacities are very much connected to living in a secure, nourishing, and joyful community. ... The voice of the spirit that urges us to care for one another is more likely to be heard when we have enough to eat and drink, and a decent place to live, and when we are in good health. We are more likely to have enough to eat, have good health care, have peace, justice, equality when we are in touch with those powerful and mysterious impulses to dedicate ourselves to the creation of a world that is true, good, and beautiful.[2]

Throughout our careers as teachers, it is important both to teach with conviction and to strive to be exemplary in our actions toward students. Whether we are teaching the multiplication tables or discussing the ethical implications of political interactions, we should promote an understanding that crosses socio-economic barriers. We should act in a compassionate manner that recognizes there is a standard by which we can interact, by which we can observe, and by which we can transform. For ourselves and for our students let us see, let us feel, let us *make a difference.*

A deeper sense of self is the feeling that I bring back from overseas and which I try to convey to my students. No one, I believe, can remain untouched by the experience of going to a rural village in Cambodia and seeing children helping other children whose legs have been blown off by a land mine get to their classroom. No one can remain untouched by the experience of going to Nigeria or Uganda or the Central African Republic and passing frail children begging for water; or going to Brazil or

Peru and watching children die from dysentery or other common diseases for the lack of a dollar's worth of medicine. These images go beyond all borders and take away all boundaries, leaving you with the realization that we are truly one people who suffer or grow as one entity, uplifted by compassion and understanding. If I can convey these feelings, thoughts, deeds and events to the children in my classroom, and have them act upon them, then I won't simply be replicating a standardized citizenship, but instead will be helping nurture the human spirit. I do not have to strive to create this, I just have to allow the spirit which we all possess to emerge — the same spirit that lights the morning, creates the tides, and enables us to be benefactors of our universe, the same spirit that moves us from deep inside to engage in service to humankind. Engaged Service *is* Compassion. As Ram Dass stated:

> Compassion in action is paradoxical and mysterious. It is absolute, yet continually changing. It accepts that everything is happening exactly as it should, and it works with a full-hearted commitment to change. It sets goals but knows that the process is all there is. It is joyful in the midst of suffering and hopeful in the face of overwhelming odds. It is simple in a world of complexity and confusion. It is done for others but nurtures the self. … Compassion is bringing our deepest truth into our actions, no matter how much the world seems to resist, because that is ultimately what we have to give this world and one another. [3]

These principles are brightening cities once blighted by squalor. Hands are reaching out to others who lack the sense of movement, smiles are creating kindness in turmoil and abuse. Envision a situation where children can be children again. I see the restoration of wilderness areas because humanity realizes at last that all ecology is one and that posterity resides within our children. I see children helping the elderly and those with Alzheimer's, as they make paper figures together, assist them with moving, read them stories, and bring them hot meals. Even very young children can help in hospitals, hospices, and other care facilities. They can help by simply being themselves, sharing their innocence and faith that "life" can be better simply by trying. As the Dalai Lama reflected in prayer:

> May I become at all times, both now and forever
> A protector of those without protection
> A guide for those who have lost their way
> A ship for those with oceans to cross
> A bridge for those with rivers to cross
> A sanctuary for those in danger
> A lamp for those without light
> A place of refuge for those who lack shelter
> And a servant to all in need. [4]

We can build houses and shelters for those who have none. We can create homes for the homeless, protection from the storm, and personal space for those who have only known the streets as the beast of chaos. If children can selflessly help other children on and off buses, to touch the sand, feel the water, or honor the wind and breeze as it caresses their face, then we will have created a curriculum that is dedicated, not to rudimentary knowledge, but to the creative force within each one of us. When we accomplish these things, then we truly have an educational system dedicated to learning and the realization of a higher calling.

If you want to stimulate a deeper sense of self within your students, look to the pockets of poverty, look to the have-nots. Guide your children in the exploration of these areas through field trips, the internet, school partnership programs, international counterparts, and the inspiration of their own hearts. By doing so, you affirm what I feel is most important for children: creating a sense of connection. With this, they have the opportunity to shift their perception of life from one of survival or mere existence to one of hope and regeneration. They find the tools to improve their lives by broadening and reframing their experiences. As Devall and Sessions point out:

Spiritual growth, or unfolding, begins when we cease to understand or see ourselves as isolated and narrow competing egos and begin to identify with other humans, from our family and friends to, eventually, our species. A nurturing non-dominating society can help in the "real work" of becoming a whole person. The "real work" can be summarized symbolically as the realization of "self-in-Self," where "Self" stands for organic wholeness. ... Biocentric equality is intimately related to the all-inclusive Self-realization in the sense that if we harm the rest of Nature then we are harming ourselves. There are no boundaries and everything is interrelated. [5]

Look to the Children

Look to the children and they will show us the way. Ask them what they need, do not explain to them what they want. Ask them how they can help, do not tell them what is required. Make the subject of the day a life that can be enhanced. Allow children to dream, allow children to run free, allow children to have their own answers to complex questions. Approach learning in an interdisciplinary manner that links body, mind, heart and soul. As Michael Murphy states:

We need to develop integral practices, which I define as transformative practices that address the somatic, affective, cognitive, volitional, and transpersonal dimensions of human nature in a comprehensive way. ... If we focus on our inter-development and bring forth our extraordinary capacities, we can learn to live more lightly on the earth, conserve the World's precious resources, and find meaning and delight through an inner-directed, more compassionate approach to life. [6]

This can be done through a multitude of activities. We must look to the children for our answers. We must integrate their voices into our process of education. We must teach that violence is not a solution as much as we teach the history of the Civil War. The understanding of sentence structure should be no more important than the realization that peace and prosperity on Earth are our consummate goals. If we understand the functions of the physical body, we must be able to understand that starvation in Rwanda, the Balkans, or India is abhorrent and unacceptable. If we understand that a grade point average is important to get into a chosen institution of higher learning, we must be able to understand that compassionate reasoning, integral learning, spiritual quests, and a sense of the sacred create what truly is the essence of the human spirit.

Throughout my life, my love of education has joined with my love of people to teach me that there are abundant opportunities for learning and growth. I find the beauty and depth of indigenous cultures around the world as fulfilling and exciting as the most celebrated museums, the most diverse art galleries, and the latest technological advancements. I feel as much joy in seeing children with limited means rolling in the grass, swimming in ponds, or hugging one another as I do with well-dressed children playing in the park. I believe that we are all conceived as a vehicle of beauty and a conveyance of good. Transformation happens every day, in every moment, whether or not we are conscious of it. It can start with ourselves and continue with our students, or it can start with our students and continue with ourselves. It is something we can work on every day, starting with ourselves, and continuing with our students. A solitary act of kindness can lead to outcomes beyond our greatest expectation. We must hold the intent to be the best practitioners that we can be. By being ourselves and living in integrity and truth, we can positively influence all whom we touch.

In conclusion, we need to create new patterns in education: patterns that convey and encourage the good of all people; patterns that make learning something students want to participate in; patterns based on a philosophy of hope rather than fear, on initiative rather than force, on love rather than hate. In order to do this, we must look to ourselves. Then we must look to each other and to the children. As Stephanie Chase foresaw:

> Children of the earth, come out of the darkness — light your candles from the stars. ... Keep vigil for all the world. Let

no heart deny the other ... let your love be the sign of peace made visible.[7]

We must look to the heavens. We must look to the earth. We must look within. The answer is in us. The answer is us. We are the solution. I pray that we may all be an active force for educational change, and find that deeper sense of self from which all is possible.

FOOTNOTES:

[1]   Gill, W. (1989). Proper Behavior for the 21st Century in our Global Village. *Middle School Journal*, p. 20.

[2]   Purpel, D.E. (1989). *The Moral and Spiritual Crisis in Education: A Curriculum for Justice and Compassion in Education*, p. 25.

[3]   Dass, R. and Bush, Mirabai (1992). *Compassion in Action: Setting Out on the Path of Service*, pp. 3-5.

[4]   Dalai Lama (1999). *Ethics for the New Millennium*, p. 237.

[5]   Deval, B. and Sessions, G. (1985). *Deep Ecology: Living as if Nature Mattered*, pp. 66-67

[6]   Murphy, M. (1993). "Integral Practices: Body, Heart and Mind" in Roger Walsh and Frances Vaughn (Eds.), *Paths Beyond Ego: The Transpersonal Vision*, pp. 171-173.

[7]   Chase, S. in Crowell, S., Caine, Renate N., and Caine, Geoffrey (1998). *The Re-Enchantment of Learning*.

XIX

The Hilltop Elementary School Story

by Thomas Lickona

In the early 1990s, Hilltop Elementary School, located in a suburb of Seattle, faced a trend that schools across the country were seeing: growing student disrespect for both adults and peers.

Geri Branch, principal at the time, recalls, "The pressure was on me to be tougher and meaner. But we began to realize that this was a far deeper issue than discipline. We needed to change the idea of what students considered 'cool' — from disrespectful to respectful."

Then Branch read a book on educating for character and offered copies to every interested teacher to read over the summer break. When the faculty returned in September, they decided to pursue character education as the best way to change the culture of their school.

Six years later, in 1999, Hilltop was one of seven elementary schools in the country to be named a National School of Character. Branch and her staff described eleven components as central to their work.

The Eleven Components

1. *Strong parent involvement.* Parents were invited to evening meetings to get their response to the idea of becoming "a school of character" and were enthusiastic about this focus. Hilltop

subsequently invited each family to volunteer in a classroom for two hours per week (75 percent now do). Parents have received weekly letters from the principal and classroom teachers, including suggestions on how to foster a particular virtue with their children at home. When Hilltop teachers retire, both students and their parents are now invited to the farewell appreciation ceremony. Parents say they are grateful to be included.

2. *Building a caring school community.* Hilltop's motto is: "We are here to learn, to love, to care, to share, and to grow — together." Branch explained:

> We want all of our students to feel valued and connected. As part of that, we try to make sure that every child has a friend in our school. We work on the goal of building community in every classroom. As a school, we now begin each academic year with what we call our New Year's Day Assembly. We introduce new staff and new students. We celebrate being back together as a family. We review school-wide rules regarding respect and responsibility and safety. We ask the children to think about and write down the goals they will work on during the coming school year.

Hilltop nurtures cross-age caring relationships through its buddy system, which pairs an older class with a younger one. The principal also makes an effort to get to know every child personally through her Friday "lunch with the principal." On that day, she eats lunch in her office with thirty-six students, two from each classroom, twelve at a time in three different groups. She says, "I use this time to talk with children about their accomplishments, their interests inside and outside school, and also about the virtues."

3. *Class meetings.* A Hilltop teacher says, "The class meeting is the backbone of our program." Branch elaborated:

> Our teachers use the class meeting to help children get to know each other. We do community-building activities

throughout the year to help students discover their similarities and differences, likes and dislikes. We use class meetings for paying each other compliments. We use them to discuss how we live together and set up rules. We use them to teach conversation skills such as active listening and looking at the person who's speaking. And we use them to empower children to be problem solvers. If there's a problem with cliques on the playground, or if people are leaving a mess in the classroom after doing projects, those are issues for a class meeting. We ask, "How can we work together to solve this problem?"

Hilltop considered class meetings such an important part of its program that all teachers attended training sessions on how to conduct them. Teachers vary in the meeting format they use and in how often they hold them; some do them daily, others as the need arises. But the expectation is that all staff will use them to intentionally teach the virtues and to give students the experience of democratic participation.

4. *Reflection.* Teachers typically do "reflection time" for the last few minutes of the school day, during which time students use a "levels of responsibility" chart to evaluate their behavior. Teachers say this time helps children hold themselves and each other accountable to high standards.

Faculty meetings are conducted in a circle to promote a sense of community and good participation. In these meetings, faculty continually reflects on Hilltop's programs, especially the character education effort. Counselor Linda Babin observed, "Reflection at our school has been transformational for both kids and adults. For kids, it helps them to really internalize the virtues. For adults, it enables us to ask, 'What's working? Where are the problem spots?'"

5. *A social skills approach to discipline.* "We now focus on discipline as something we do with our students, not to them," Branch said. "When it comes to discipline, you have to look past what kids are doing and find out why they're doing it. We

want them to understand why they should behave in a certain way. When they understand that, behavior is much more likely to change."

About 75 percent of Hilltop's approach to discipline is now proactive, teaching social skills.

> We practice manners — saying "please" and "thank you," holding the door for someone coming behind you — all of the time, everywhere in the building. Manners are the glue of our relationships. Visitors always comment on the good manners of our students.
>
> We teach children to make "I statements," for example, "I didn't like it when you did that because ... ," so that they are able to express their anger in a safe way.
>
> We teach a strategy for solving conflicts: *Stop, think,* and *plan.* Ask, what is the problem? What are some possible solutions? Would a particular solution be fair? Would it work? How would people feel about it? After you try the solution, ask yourself: Is it working? If not, what else could I try? We also do a lot of mediation, helping kids work things out.

6. *The Window Room.* A unique part of Hilltop's approach to discipline is its multipurpose Window Room, a bright, sunny room staffed by two educational assistants with involvement and supervision by the school counselor. Initially, students were referred to the Window Room just for negative behavior, but now they come for a variety of reasons:

> *Cool-down time.* When a staff member is upset with a student's behavior, or when a student is upset about something, the Window Room can be a place for cooling off and getting back to appropriate choices and behavior. Depending on the circumstances, the supervising adult may ask the student to write about what occurred, perhaps offering an apology.
>
> *Interpersonal problem solving.* Students may come alone or with another person to discuss a conflict they're having. Sometimes an adult guides the student(s) in working out a solution; sometimes they work it out on their own.
>
> *Emotional support.* Some students come to seek emotional support from an adult regarding a problem they might be

having at school or home. Some students are scheduled for weekly one-on-one time with an adult.

Quiet work space. Some students come to the Window Room to find a quiet place to work, away from all distractions.

Alternative to recess. Rather than outdoor recess, many students choose to come to the Window Room to play games, read, do artwork, or just talk to each other.

Positive reinforcement. Staff sometimes sends students to the Window Room in appreciation of especially positive behavior or commendable performance in the classroom.

In-school suspension. Occasionally, a misbehaving student is sent to the Window Room as a place to complete assigned work away from the classroom.

7. *The Justice Committee.* Hilltop's Justice Committee, like the class meeting, teaches students the democratic process. This committee has the job of dealing with school problems that haven't been solved through other school procedures. The principal oversees the committee; students in grades four through six are eligible to serve. Service is considered a responsibility of school citizenship, similar to jury duty. Teachers randomly choose a different student from their classroom every three weeks to take a turn. A student or staff member can present a problem for consideration, and the Justice Committee brainstorms possible solutions. Recommended solutions are then presented to the principal for approval.

For example, Hilltop students typically take a portion of their lunch outside for recess. Litter on the school grounds was making a lot of extra work for the custodian. He took his concern to the Justice Committee, which recommended that all classrooms discuss this problem. The outcome was a schoolwide renewal of the commitment to keeping the grounds clean.

8. *A monthly focus.* "For the first three years of our program," Branch said, "we focused only on respect and responsibility. After a while, it began to sound too routine. We tried doing three virtues a year. That still didn't give us enough momentum. So

we went to nine virtues, one a month, with building respect and responsibility as the integrating theme."

September:	Perseverance/hard work
October:	Cooperation/sportsmanship
November:	Service/citizenship
December:	Kindness/caring
January:	Tolerance
February:	Fairness/justice
March:	Courage
April:	Trustworthiness/honesty
May:	Self-discipline

9. *Curricular integration.* Hilltop's faculty regularly integrates character education into reading, writing, social studies, and physical education. One common approach is teaching the virtues through discussing stories, both fictional and those found in the daily newspaper. (Sample assignment: "Be looking for examples in the paper of kindness or cruelty; bring those in to share with the class.") Picture books like *The Empty Pot* (about a boy who had the courage to appear before the emperor with the empty truth) have proved to be a good source of character lessons, and so have chapter books such as *The Witch of Blackbird Pond* and *Roll of Thunder, Hear My Cry.*

Many teachers have students write about the qualities they admire in famous historical and contemporary figures ("I admire Sally Ride because ..."). One teacher explains, "I move from the study of famous figures to having kids write about their own talents and character strengths. We also bring in multiple intelligences: Are they strong in musical intelligence? Artistic intelligence? Social intelligence? And so on."

Hilltop teachers say that integrating character education has made academic subject matter more meaningful and motivating for children.

10. *Recognition.* "Many schools rely on extrinsic rewards to motivate good behavior," Branch says, "but we think that can be

counter-productive. As a society, we suffer from a preoccupation with 'What will I get for doing this?'" Hilltop stresses social recognition rather than material rewards. Branch commented:

> We are constantly paying attention to positive behavior. If a student holds a door, I'll say, "Thank you for holding the door. That was a very thoughtful thing to do." They're not doing it so much to please you but because they are connected to you. They value the relationship. That's why taking the time to build caring relationships is so important.

Hilltop also has Celebration Assemblies. These recognize students by giving them the opportunity to perform — to do musical recitals, skits, plays, and readings of poems and stories, many of which highlight the virtue of the month. Student performances are then repeated at community events, other schools, and nursing homes.

At the close of the school year, Hilltop has hosted its own Character Education Conference, often with a nationally known presenter. Other schools in the district, and sometimes beyond, are invited to attend. The afternoon includes recognition and appreciation of all the things Hilltop staff do to make the character education program a success.

11. *Nurturing transitions.* In the past few years, because of retirements and moves, Hilltop has experienced a turnover in approximately half its staff, including bringing on a new principal, Penny Smith. In some schools, staff turnover and especially the departure of a strong principal have spelled the undoing of a character education program. But Hilltop has stayed the course. Counselor Linda Babin says, "In order to support new staff coming on board, we have held monthly meetings to discuss character education strategies and the foundational philosophy underlying our approach to character education. Our new staff have told us that they feel warmly welcomed and supported and that they can see the high level of teamwork and cooperation that goes on among all our staff." Since Hilltop began its character education program, it has seen not only improvement

in students' behavior but also a slow, steady rise in their standardized test scores. Moreover, on a district School Climate Survey, Hilltop ranked above the average in thirty-eight of the forty indicators.

What stands out in the Hilltop story? Two things, both stemming from the principal's thoughtful leadership: the emphasis on community and the emphasis on reflection. No character education program I know of makes the quality of human relationships more central. The priority attached to developing a caring school community pervades everything Hilltop does. When I visited Hilltop a few years ago, the warmth and caring of the school were something you could almost reach out and touch.

No school recognized for character education excellence spends more time on reflection. Hilltop's motto could be, "The unexamined life is not worth living." Class meetings examine the quality of collective life. End-of-the-day "reflection time" examines the level of respect and responsibility exhibited by class members during that day. Academic instruction examines the virtues as they appear in literature, history, current events, and other subjects. The handling of discipline, including the Window Room, gets children to reflect on the reasons underlying a behavior problem they're having and how to solve it. Faculty devotes half of their regular meetings to sharing what they're doing in character education and how they can do it better.

These days, time for reflection is an increasingly scarce commodity in schools, especially with mounting pressures from the standards and testing movements. But without reflection time for both students and staff, quality character education is impossible to achieve. Creating a culture of character requires that all school members continually think and talk about how to make the virtues a living matter. Hilltop exemplifies how to do that.

PART FOUR

The Students

*Never can children's education be complete
unless we impart in them a true appreciation
of the eternal values of life.*

Swami Chinmayananda

Each second we live is a new and unique moment of the universe, a moment that will never be again. ... And what do we teach our children? We teach them that two and two make four, and that Paris is the capital of France. When will we also teach them what they are? We should say to each of them: Do you know what you are? You are a marvel. You are unique.

In all the years that have passed, there has never been another child like you. Your legs, your arms, your clever fingers, the way you move. You may become a Shakespeare, a Michaelangelo, and a Beethoven. You have the capacity for anything. Yes, you are a marvel. And when you grow up, can you then harm another who is, like you, a marvel? You must work—we must all work—to make the world worthy of its children.

Pablo Casals

XX

The Purpose of Values

by Swami Tejomayananda

We find that virtues and values alone add beauty to our lives. And we all enjoy beauty. We want our houses and our surroundings to be beautiful, and we also want to look beautiful. But please remember that there is not only an outer visual attractiveness but there is a factor called inner beauty as well. We may be fascinated by outer beauty and our initial attraction may be because of that, but we soon discover that appearances can be deceptive. Someone may appear beautiful on the outside, but when we come to live with that person, life becomes impossible. What is that inner beauty? What is it that draws us to certain people even when they are old or handicapped, or not at all physically attractive? It is a fact that these people possess special inner qualities of good character and virtue. So in simple terms, values and virtues make our lives more beautiful.

We should recognize that whenever we want to achieve a particular goal in life we need both the outer means as well as the inner resources of values and virtues. The outer means that we need may vary with the particular goal. For example, as students we want to pass with good grades. As businessmen we want to be prosperous. As housewives we want our home to be clean and comfortable. But whatever our goal may be, the inner resources that we need remain the same. We need physical energy to work hard, and we need mental energy to support and sustain that activity.

Just as economics is the science for managing money and finances there is also a science of economizing the expenditure of our energy, avoiding unnecessary dissipation of one's inner vitality. This is known as the science of spirituality. It is with a wealth of inner virtues that we ensure success in reaching our goals. Generally we find that a lot of our energy is dissipated even before we start a project. We already feel tired before we begin. So, one way of conserving energy is by being honest. Some people cannot tell the truth no matter what. They are manipulative and say different things to different people. That puts them under constant pressure to remember what they told to whom, so that their dishonesty will not show. When a person is truthful, however, he has nothing to worry about.

It is said that when Mahatma Gandhi was in England, he appeared to be quite relaxed before a big press conference. Many political leaders are under great stress at such times and spend days preparing for these events. The Mahatma's secretary asked him how he could remain so relaxed. Gandhiji promptly responded that he had nothing to hide; he just had to tell the truth and present the facts as they were. Honesty was the secret to his tranquil state. Life is simple when we do not try to manipulate. When we practice good values, the energy that it brings into our life is tremendous!

Another way to conserve energy is to manage our time well. We can achieve maximum work in minimum time if we are disciplined. Otherwise there is always work pending and we are under stress trying to catch up with our commitments. For example, if a student is given a project and he procrastinates, then just days before the project is due, he will get into a panic. When our activities are on time and under control, we feel free. There is no stress and no dissipation of mental energy.

A third value that saves energy is orderliness. "A place for everything and everything in its place!" Otherwise, as in some homes, every morning begins with a hunting expedition. First we try to find the keys. Then the search for the portable phone begins. We become agitated and so does everyone else. The entire household begins looking for that one object. These are simple matters, but how much time and energy would be saved if things were kept in their respective places! There are so many creative activities that we can participate in if we learn to manage our time and energy.

What is the difference between an ordinary and an extraordinary person? And how does one become an extraordinary person? It is not that the extraordinary person suddenly drops down from the heavens. They become who they are by simply living what they have learned. And that one simple fact lifts them to those great heights. Both ordinary as well as extraordinary people can have the same amount of knowledge. One acts on what he knows and matures from it, while the ordinary person, despite book knowledge remains at the same level, without any change. But when we see someone achieve great things, we see that this person adheres to certain principles and values, which make him a great person. For example, some people are good artists but they lack discipline and that is the only reason they do not become successful. This is of vital importance but we ignore it. We perform so many actions, but by ignoring the value system we are missing the joy that we should be experiencing in life. The divine virtues bring joy and happiness not only to us, but also to others.

Don't take any job just for the money. Money is an automatic byproduct if you are good at what you do. Take a job to serve people so everyone can benefit. If you want to become an engineer, dream of building the best structures. When you serve others you will never compromise with your values. It is when you work only for money that you may compromise your values to make more money. See what happened in the Indian state of Gujarat during the earthquake. Some say builders did not plan the buildings well enough or build them strong enough to face earthquakes. Whatever you want to become, dream of serving as much as possible. Money will automatically come but real satisfaction will come from your service.

Swami Swaaropananda

XXI

Immortal Values

by Swami Chinmayananda

Civilization flourishes with the promotion of culture, but when the cultural values deteriorate, the civilization of a society breaks down, as we have known from the fall of Egyptian, Greek, and Roman civilizations. The great religious masters of India, using their own ingenious efforts, have time and again revived the philosophical and religious values, for which India stood, and thereby arrested the deterioration of the culture. When culture deteriorates, there is an increase in barbarity and immorality in the country, and its philosophy misinterpreted, leading to confusion and chaos among its people. This, in short, is more or less the sad condition of the present world. The need of the hour is to arrest forthwith the deterioration by reviving the great philosophical and religious values of life.

In no other literature in the world have these values been so beautifully and exhaustively dealt with as in the sacred books of India. In this context we may note the following advice given to the students by the rishi of the *Taittirīya Upaniṣad*:

> The practice of what is right and proper is fixed by the scriptural texts; it is to be followed along with reading the texts oneself and propagating the truths of the same. ["Truths": this means that practicing in life what is understood to be right and proper is to be pursued along with regular studies and preaching.] Penance, study, and preaching; control of the senses, study, and preaching; tranquility, study, and preaching; the "maintenance of fire," study, and preaching; offering

to fire in fire-sacrifice, study, and preaching of the Vedas; procreation, study, and preaching; propagation of the race, study, and preaching — all these are things to be practiced sincerely.

Satyavachas, son of Rathitara, holds that Truth alone is to be strictly practiced. Tapanitya, son of Paurusisti, declares that penance alone is to be practiced. Naka, son of Mudgala, holds the view that the study and preaching of the Vedas only are to be practiced; that verily is penance: aye, that is penance. (I: 9)

This portion of the *Upaniṣad* represents the last concluding lecture given by the teacher to the students of Vedanta in their classroom as they are about to leave for home from the *gurukula* they had studied in for some years. In the ancient tradition called the *gurukula* system, the students lived together with the teacher during the length of study, becoming part of the teacher's family. This Upanishadic passage closely parallels the corresponding function that we have in our colleges today, which goes by the term "convocation address." The students are given some key ideas on how they should live lives dedicated to their culture, consistent with what has been taught to them as the goal and way of life.

More Than Just Facts

It must be the duty of the educationists to see that they impart to the growing generation not merely some factual knowledge or some wondrous theories but also ideals of pure living, and training in how to live those ideals in practical life. In short, the secret of a sound culture is crystallized in this convocation address; this portion is more exhaustively amplified in the section that follows the address.

In this section the teacher presents twelve immortal ideas of living and rules of conduct. An equal number of times he has insisted that the student continue his study of the scriptures and propagate the immortal ideas of his culture all through his life. In these passages, we find that the brilliant students are repeatedly commissioned to continue their study and be preachers throughout their lifetime. The Upanishadic style lies in its brevity. Use of even a syllable more than the minimum required is considered as a great sin; yet, here we find in a small section twelve repetitions of the same idea: study (*svādhyāya*) and discoursing upon the Veda with a view to making others understand (*pravacana*).

For this missionary work the rishis never saw any necessity for organizing a special class of teachers. The preaching activity was built into the duty of every householder. In the pursuit of his vocation, the householder was not asked to spare any special time or to sacrifice his duties either toward himself, or toward his own children, the society, the nation, or the world. But while emphasizing the need for pursuing his duties at all these levels, the rishis asked him to keep continuously in touch with the scriptures and to preach the same truth to others.

The great qualities that the teacher has insisted upon are: (a) the practice of what is right and proper as indicated in the scriptures (*ṛtaṁ*); (b) living up to the ideals that have been intellectually comprehended during the studies (*satyam*); (c) a spirit of self-sacrifice and self-denial (*tapas*); (d) control of the senses (*dama*); (e) tranquility of the mind (*sama*); (f) maintenance of a charitable and ready kitchen at home in the service of all deserving hungry fellow beings (*agni*); (g) practice of concentration and ritualism through fire-worship as was in vogue in the society of those days; and (h) doing one's duty toward humanity, toward one's children and grandchildren, and toward society.

At the end of the section, three great masters are quoted who had in the past declared the most important of the above. The necessary quality to be cultivated according to each is either *satyam* or *tapas* or study of the *śāstra* and their efficient spread in the society (*svādhyāya pravacana*).

In short, the section reads as a manifesto upon the ideal way of living, in which every person is charged to live true to his or her own intellectual convictions (*satyam*), in a spirit of self-denial (*tapas*), while attending to the study of the sacred texts (*svādhyāya*) and to the spread of culture among the peoples of the world (*pravacana*), not merely by preaching but also by living the very same virtues and values in his or her own private life. Therefore, continuing the "convocation address," the teacher says:

> Having taught the Vedas, the preceptor enjoins the pupil: "Speak the truth, do your duty, never swerve from the study of the Vedas; do not cut off the line of descendants in your family, after giving the preceptor the *guru dakṣiṇā*. Never deviate from truth, never fail in your duty, never overlook your own welfare, never neglect your prosperity, never neglect the study and the propagation of the Vedas." (I:11)

After the studies, before the students are let out to meet their destinies in their independent individual life as social beings, the teacher gives his exhortation, which comprises, we might say, "Vedanta in practice." The entire wealth of knowledge gained by the rishi in their experiments with the world of objects, the world of thoughts, and the world of ideas has been brought from the temples and libraries to the home and the fields.

The modern, half-educated youth are tempted to cry down Vedanta as an impractical theory; this can be the sad moaning of only those who have not read this portion — the crystallized essence of Hinduism — with sufficient poise and peaceful reflection.

It is the very nature of the human heart, especially when it is young, to aspire for some ideal to follow, some great aspiration from which to draw all inspirations. No education is complete without the heart discovering an inspiring goal for itself, with which it can surge forward and achieve greatness in its lifetime. Once this ideal has been gathered, thereafter, very readily, all our vital energies — intellectual, physical, and mental — will spontaneously pour out with a purposeful dash into the chosen field of our life's soaring ambitions. Without such an aspiration, goal or purpose, life becomes empty and even the best amongst us cannot discover any extra brilliance about our existence. To help the youth to discover such a salient goal is the very be-all and end-all of all education. Without this, all our studies can only add up to mere instructions and data mongering.

Swami Chinmayananda

XXII

The Debt We Owe
Our Teachers

by Michael Higgins

Anyone who has ever studied in the academy, at whatever level, knows the significant, indeed determinative, role that can be played by a good teacher.

This is a point sanely argued by the firmly conservative American Jesuit political scientist, James Schall, in his irritating but wonderfully readable, *On the Unseriousness of Human Affairs* (2001), when he notes that the greatest shapers of civilization have been teachers: Socrates and Jesus.

Few of us can claim tutors of such magnitude, but we all know teachers, mentors, role-models who have had a critical influence on the making of our character, career choice, or life-long intellectual and spiritual passions.

We treasure them because they are so few and their impact so great. And enduring.

For me, the recent death of George Sanderson, a professor emeritus in the department of philosophy at St. Francis Xavier University [STFX] in Antigonish, N.S., brought home in a poignant way the debt we owe our teachers.

Sanderson was more than a mentor; he was a friend of many decades. He taught me a senior course in philosophy that dealt with contemporary issues, that was Socratic rather than magisterial in its style and approach, and that eschewed the timidity characteristic of most Thomistic methodologies employed by philosophy departments in Catholic universities in the 1960s by welcoming far-ranging discussions around epistemological and metaphysical matters that weren't safely sifted through the sieve of scholasticism.

Because of George, we read Henri Bergson and Marshall McLuhan; we talked about Freud and Husserl; and we wrestled with "being" and shifting human paradigms. In other words, he taught us to think.

But running through all his intellectual questing — he began as a geology student at McGill moved on to philosophy at STFX courtesy of fellow Montrealer Warren Allmand and ended up with a doctorate from Louvain in Belgium — George nurtured, as we would now say, his spiritual side.

He was an intellectual who took faith seriously, in his research interests, in his writing and editing (he was for many years editor of the award-winning literary and cultural periodical *The Antigonish Review*), in his life as a faculty member and professor, and in his family life.

He refused to be bifurcated: scholar versus man of faith; each supported and defined the other. He was of a piece.

I last saw him in March of last year [2005] when I was giving an invited lecture to the STFX community titled "Five Quirky Things: An Enchirdion (handbook) for the Wise."

Afterwards, he pointedly reminded me that, although he enjoyed the lecture, it was a bit longer than those he experienced when he was my teacher. I got the point. He always made sure I got the point.

He suggested we co-edit a work that would compile a selection of religious poetry of the highest order including Gerard Manley Hopkins, Robert Lowell, Geoffrey Hill, John Berryman and Thomas Merton, a work he dubbed "a portable, puissant potpourri of pensées," a secular breviary that would "appeal to believers who want to reflect and deepen their religious sensibility and to secular seekers who are open to the religious dimension."

I thought the project a splendid one and I welcomed the opportunity to work with an esteemed teacher.

Death, however, intervened. But the proposal was vintage Sanderson: open to the world, non judgmental, Catholic at its best. R.B. MacDonald, a former dean of arts at STFX, and a priest-academic of impressive integrity, captured something of the essential Sanderson in his funeral homily when he showcased not only George's holy sagacity and communitarian instincts but his self-deprecating sense of humor:

> George was, as would be said in ages past, a "character." Indeed, the occasional iconoclast is always welcomed. When the Congregation in the Vatican curia in charge of liturgy removed St. George from the official martyrology, George said that it didn't really matter that the church no longer believed in St. George, but it was important that dragons do.

The perfect quip and so like George.

XXIII

A Reflection on Education

by Kartikay Mehrotra

Learning is a lifelong process. Although formal systems of education are available to nearly every individual, the concept of education stretches far beyond textbooks, lesson plans, and classrooms. In fact, practical application of one's thoughts, whether they are learned or instinctive, provides for a more valuable education than any lesson in a classroom.

A child's understanding of education is limited to formal enrollment in a public or private institution. For most K-12 students, going to school followed by reinforcement of the concepts discussed in class is the extent to which education is defined. Repetition of an idea until ingrained in the mind through homework assignments, in-class lessons and examinations provide children with some tools for life and a basis for conceptual understanding applied in higher education. But life's educational process has little to do with formulas and facts.

I spent my childhood in a place where the education youngsters were receiving was touted as one of the best public education systems in the United States. Brighton Central School District in Rochester, NY offered more Advanced Placement classes, more teachers per student and more opportunities outside the classroom than the vast majority of other public districts in the nation. Although I must give my formal education credit for teaching me how to read and write, districts like BCSD can cause more harm than good to impressionable minds.

In grade school, competition was a frequent teaching mechanism used to encourage young minds to strive for higher standards. In my English and mathematics classes, teachers always announced the best grade in the class and made it a point to acknowledge extraordinary success. The best time achieved in gym class or the highest grade on the class project were glorified and posted on bulletin boards for months to come.

Achieving the highs and hitting the lows shined light on how this means of progress could be troublesome. Not only did it glorify the individual, it denied attention to insecure children who desperately sought opportunity. The educational limelight did provide children with a taste of what the result of hard work could provide, but competition against others does not provide a stable and accurate example of progress.

Rather, the competition within one's self to become better, at whatever given task, provides a firm basis for growth in the future. Pushing the mind to think faster and smarter, to be more efficient and to think logically and critically at the same time is an even greater challenge, one which has guided me to meet a higher standard than competing for the highest grade in the class.

"Someone will always be better than you," a phrase I've heard many times by individuals actually trying to encourage my own abilities. Such a statement could be misunderstood to be discouraging, but it is also a simple truth. If we are a society which, hopefully, is progressing to reach higher standards, then we must come to terms with the limits of our own abilities and the ability of others to improve upon them. The statement also implies that competition against others is not the provider of growth in an individual. But rather, the competition against one's self to improve upon past experiences will improve one's abilities as well as character.

In high school and the early part of college I again fell victim to the powers of competition and stumbled in achieving my potential. Though I cannot blame the system for my shortcomings, I cannot help but think that if I had been introduced to practical application beyond word-problems in math class, I would have more to offer society by this point in my life.

My understanding of education changed during a six-month hiatus from college when I served as an intern for a local news and talk radio station in Chicago. As an intern, my expectations to produce were minimal. The professional journalists and broadcasters wanted me to take in as much as I could without mucking-up-the-works. I tried to make the most of that experience by traveling with reporters and playing the role of journalist. I gained invaluable knowledge about how to present myself as a professional and how to think critically when speaking to a politician. Those are two attributes that I would never learn in a classroom, but only through practical experience attained because I wanted to become a better journalist; a competition within myself.

My experience at the radio station taught me more than any class or lesson-plan. By no means is that intended to slight my teachers. In fact, they acknowledge that practical experience is a highly constructive way of improving one's abilities. Although a classroom remains the venue for the understanding of basics, an individual's desire to improve is the true platform for progress.

When I was a child, the concept of learning from my mistakes was never more than a cliché. I simply had not spent enough time living to think about my childish mistakes and misconceptions, or their impact. Yet one of the lessons that seems to have stuck in my mind was the concept of learning from my mistakes. Perhaps because it was emphasized through many different venues, Bal-Vihar (children's cultural classes offered by Chinmaya Mission), sports, school, music, or family life, the concept has stayed with me until finally ringing true. When taking on a new task, like a brand new career, I have tried to apply what I learned through my formal education and practical experience. The lessons which jump out at me first are the ones I learned from mistakes I have made.

Education is not the process of sitting in a classroom and listening to a teacher lecture. It is the actual act of learning, however it may be done. It is a means of personal growth and even a process of life. Education is the experience one accumulates in life. The most valuable experiences are the ones an individual can learn from and then apply to the future. In the short run, these actions are often deemed to be mistakes, but as one progresses in life, they will become defining moments of understanding and even clarity. While applying the lessons I have learned from the past, I will make more mistakes; they are unavoidable. I can only hope to learn from them and apply them as progress in life.

XXIV

Becoming Quality Leaders

by Azim Premji

[Following is a Convocation Address given by Mr. Premji on October 10, 2004 to the Sahodaya School Complexes in Bangalore]

Ladies and Gentlemen: I have always believed that the "power to decide" must be left to those who are closest to action. In education, this power must be vested with the teachers, the students, the parents, and the schools. This gathering represents a commendable effort by the Central Board of Secondary Education [CBSE] to decentralize the education system and empower schools. It gives me great pleasure to be invited to participate in this effort.

Let me begin by talking to you about one issue that is really very important. As I look to the future, I see enormous opportunity for India in the global arena. According to various reports I get from time to time, India has the potential of becoming one of the top economies in the world by 2050. But to convert this opportunity into reality, we need leaders who can face up to the challenges along the way.

What makes a good leader? Apart from sincerity and ability to work hard, good leaders are those who have an inquiring and critical mind, who are excited by challenge and are willing to take risks. Leaders need to be creative. They must be willing to collaborate and work well in teams. They must always want to learn. Leaders need to respect diversity. And most important, they must have the resilience to stand firmly by a set of values that can guide them and those who work with them.

Though many of us in the industry recruit the best people that India has to offer, we find that these characteristics are absent in many of them. The qualities I described cannot be so developed after one becomes an adult. Even if they can, it is an arduous task and their qualities do not go deep enough into the personality. These need to be developed from a tender age, when the mind is fresh and uncluttered. A dry sponge absorbs maximum water. That is why schools have the biggest role in nurturing such development. There is no doubt that our students do well in academic skills and some of them have brought great honor for our country. Yet, when it comes to a vast majority of students, we need to face the question head on: are we creating leaders or just large masses of followers who look to others to tell them what to do with their lives.

I have often wondered why is it that the best people who go through our education system sometimes do not bring basic "life" qualities to the work place. Does our obsessive focus with examination come in the way of developing an overall personality? Passing examinations cannot become the purpose of education just like crossing signals cannot be the purpose of going on a journey. This makes our education another "tuition" center. In fact, the tuition industry owes its existence to the examination mania. It is almost like one error being compounded by another by further emphasizing just one part of the person at the cost of all other parts. The end result is that in many cases we could end up by churning out standardized children like graded "products" in a factory, who remain weak in creating, thinking, discovering and learning. Such individuals are programmed to obey and conform, because they have limited life skills and need continuous direction.

I am not an Educationist but I have had the opportunity of interacting with many of the students who graduate from various institutes across the country. I wanted to share my honest thoughts with you. You may like to evaluate these in the light of your own experiences. I do hope that these thoughts will give you useful pointers to evaluate the fundamental assumptions on which we rest our education system.

So, going back to the earlier question, if passing examinations is not the sole purpose of education, then what is it that schools must aim for? In my view, schools are and must be agents of individual growth and social transformation. By individual growth, I am only reiterating the belief that every child has infinite potential. Can our schools help each child in tapping that potential? By social transformation, I am stressing the role of schools in building a certain kind of society. Until our schools care for every child and thus teach every child to care for another, we can never hope to create a truly inclusive and harmonious society.

An Ideal School

If I were to dream about an ideal school, it would be a school that believes in the child's right to respect. A school that understands that every child learns differently, at different depths and at different speeds. A school that assesses, not to judge, but to improve learning. A school that cares for children and feels responsible for the holistic progress of every child. A school that invests in teacher development, better assessment systems and community participation. A school that realizes that feeding content does not equal learning. A school that believes in helping each child construct his or her own knowledge and finally, a school that continuously learns. Can this be your school? Maybe you have even better ideas on what can make an ideal school. All I ask is that you should have your own dream, whatever it may be. We need to accept what needs to be changed to move towards that dream. A dream becomes a vision and model for action when we truly begin to believe that we have whatever it takes to achieve our dream. Then the hard work that follows to make it happen makes the journey a joy in itself.

I know that, in the last couple of years, the CBSE has made several attempts to progressively improve board exams. This has also led to many schools to change their internal assessment systems. But any change that happens at the instance of others carries only so much energy and momentum. A change that comes from inside on the other hand has no such limits because the commitment to it is total and binding.

If you are willing to make a beginning, it may be worthwhile to evaluate the assessment systems in your school. We need to ask whether they only test memory or do they check whether the child has truly understood concepts at a deeper level, and is now able to apply this learning in the real world. Test is a screen. Before we check how well it screens, we must evaluate whether it screens the right things. And the taste of the pudding lies in the eating. If the screen can measure how well the child is prepared for the life ahead; it is an appropriate screen. But if it does not, then no matter how tough the screen is, it is totally meaningless.

To give you a simple instance, instead of asking children what happened in the 1857 war of independence, could you ask them to describe, in their own words, why the war happened? And then ask them to draw out their own learning that they can apply in the real world. It is not remembering the facts alone that matters, but the ability to interpret them and use them as thinking frameworks for their own decisions.

Over the past few years, I have worked with the poorest of village schools, and I have worked with best urban schools. I have witnessed what I can call the "pyramid of aspiration." The village government school wishes to be like the village private school. The village private school wishes to be like the best private school in the nearby town. This town school wishes to be like private schools in cities like Bangalore. And, in turn, they wish to be like the "best" school around – typically, this is the neighborhood CBSE school. The Sahoday network, and each one of you here, represents the peak of that pyramid of aspirations. I think it is something to be proud about.

As leading schools, you hold the destiny of the Indian school system. If each one of you is able to transform your school into true beacons of quality, then you will see the ripple slowly moving outward to encompass the entire network of schools in the country.

I want each of you to recognize that the leadership I see in this gathering is not only a privilege and honor but also an enormous responsibility. When I look at you today, I see the future of our country right here in front of my eyes!

You owe it not only to yourself and but also to the other schools in the country to rise to the challenges and make the most of the opportunity that lies ahead. Most importantly though, you owe it to every trusting child who has placed his or her life in your hands. I am sure you will do everything possible to ensure that the child succeeds. As teachers I am sure that your overwhelming pride comes from each successful step the child takes. I can only offer gratitude to my own teachers who have helped to achieve whatever success I have had in my life. There will be many students who will recollect for years what you have done for them. I wish you all the best in the rewarding journey that lies ahead for you. Thank you.

About the Authors

Borba, Michele

Michele Borba, Ed.D., is an internationally renowned educator and award-winning author who is recognized for her practical, solution-based strategies to strengthen child's behavior, self-esteem, character, and social development, and to build strong families. A sought-after motivational speaker, she has presented workshops and keynote addresses throughout North America, Europe, Asia and the South Pacific and has served as an educational consultant to hundreds of schools, and organizations. She is the author of 21 books and lives in Palm Springs, California.

Brock, Michael L.

Michael L. Brock, M.A., a respected educator with over 25 years of experience, gives seminars throughout the country on parenting issues.

Bruchac, Joseph

Joseph Bruchac's writing draws on his Abenaki, American Indian ancestry. He holds a B.A. from Cornell University, an M.A. in Literature and Creative Writing from Syracuse and a Ph.D. in Comparative Literature from the Union Institute of Ohio. His work as an educator includes eight years of directing a college program for Skidmore College inside a maximum security prison. With his wife, Carol, he is the founder and Co-Director of the *Greenfield Review Literary Center* and *The Greenfield Review Press*. He discusses Native culture in his books and does storytelling programs at dozens of elementary and secondary schools each year as a visiting author.

Donnelly, John

John Donnelly is a Special Needs teacher in Anaheim, California. He is also Director of the International Foundation for Social and Educational Dimensions which works with schools in Europe and Asia.

Esquith, Rafe

Rafe Esquith is beginning his eighteenth year at Hobart Elementary School in Los Angeles. He is the product of the Los Angeles public schools and a graduate of UCLA. His many honors and awards include the 1992 Disney National Outstanding Teacher of the Year Award, a Sigma Beta Delta Fellowship from Johns Hopkins University, *Parents Magazine's* As You Grow Award, Oprah Winfrey's Use Your Life Award, and an MBE from Queen Elizabeth. He lives in Los Angeles with his wife, Barbara Tong.

Glenn, H. Stephen

H. Stephen Glenn, Ph.D., is the coauthor of the bestselling classic *Raising Self-Reliant Children* (Prima) and the president of Capabilities, Inc., a company that provides resources and materials for business and industry, human services, and education and family life.

Higgins, Michael

Michael Higgins has been associated with St. Jerome's University as member of the Religious Studies and English departments and served as the first Director of the St. Jerome's Centre for

Catholic Experience and as Academic Dean and Vice-President. St. Jerome's University is a public Roman Catholic university federated with the University of Waterloo. He gained national recognition for his publications and broadcast journalism, working in particular on the CBC-Radio program *Ideas* and authoring or co-authoring a number of books. He became President and Vice-Chancellor in 1999. He takes on his new responsibilities as President of St. Thomas University in July 2006.

Honoré, Carl

Carl Honoré was born in Scotland but grew up in Canada. His hometown is Edmonton, Alberta. After studying history and Italian at Edinburgh University, he worked with street children in Brazil. This inspired him to take up journalism. Since 1991, he has written from all over Europe and South America, spending three years in Buenos Aires along the way. His work has appeared in publications on both sides of the Atlantic, including the *Economist, Observer, National Post, Globe and Mail, Houston Chronicle* and *Miami Herald*. He now lives in London with his wife and two children.

Krishna, P.

Professor P. Krishna was a Professor of Physics at the Banaras Hindu University in India till 1986 and then Rector of the Krishnamurti Education Centre in Varanasi till 2003. He is presently a visiting Professor at the D.A. University in Indore, India. He is a fellow of the Indian National Science Academy, New Delhi and has lectured internationally on education, science, society, and religion. Several of his articles can be accessed at his website www.pkrishna.org

Kaneda, Takuya

Takuya Kaneda, Associate Professor of Art Education, at Otsuma Women's University in Tokyo, spent a number of years in India and Nepal doing research as well as visiting Tagore's school at Shantiniketan. He was a visiting teacher at J. Krishnamurti's Rishi Valley School in India in 1999. He has written many articles on art and education.

Lickona, Thomas

Dr. Thomas Lickona is a developmental psychologist and Professor of Education at the State University of New York at Cortland, where he has done award-winning work in teacher education and currently directs the Center for the Fourth and Fifth Rs (Respect and Responsibility). He has also been a visiting professor at Boston and Harvard Universities. A past president of the Association for Moral Education, Dr. Lickona now serves on the advisory councils of the Character Education Partnership, Character Counts Coalition, and Medical Institute for Sexual Health. Dr. Lickona has authored many books and is a frequent consultant to schools on character education and a frequent speaker at conferences for teachers, parents, religious educators, and other groups concerned about the moral development of young people. He has lectured across the United States and in Canada, Japan, Switzerland, Ireland, and Latin America on the subject of teaching moral values in the school and in the home.

Mehrotra, Kartikay

Kartikay is a 22-year-old news reporter for the *Kane County Chronicle* in Geneva, IL. He graduated from Northern Illinois University in December 2005. During his time at NIU he served as a writing consultant and wrote for the *Northern Star* and *Sun Publications*. He enjoys keeping his community informed while reporting on local governments in the growing county west of

Chicago. He enjoys being active outdoors and keeps himself entertained with music and by attending concerts.

Miller, Ron

Ron Miller is currently the Executive Editor of *Paths of Learning* magazine and President of the Foundation for Educational Renewal. Previously he was the founding editor of *Holistic Education Review* (now called *Encounter*). He is historian of alternative and progressive educational movements and has written or edited six books, including *What Are Schools For? Holistic Education in American Culture* and *Caring for New Life: Essays on Holistic Education.* He is also a co-founder of the Bellwether School near Burlington, Vermont.

The Mother

The Mother, Mirra Alfassa, was born on February 21, 1878 in Paris. In 1914 she voyaged to Pondicherry, South India, to meet the Indian mystic Sri Aurobindo, and stayed for eleven months. In April 1920 the Mother rejoined Sri Aurobindo in Pondicherry. Six years later, when the Sri Aurobindo Ashram was founded, Sri Aurobindo entrusted its material and spiritual charge to her. Under her guidance, which covered a period of nearly fifty years, the Ashram grew into a large, many-faceted spiritual community. She also established a school, the Sri Aurobindo International Centre of Education, in 1952, and an international township, Auroville, in 1968. The Mother left her body on November 17, 1973.

Noddings, Nel

Nel Noddings is among the leading figures in the field of Educational Philosophy. She is Professor of Philosophy and Education at Teachers College, Columbia University, and Lee L. Jacks Professor of Child Education Emerita at Stanford University.

Premji, Azim

Azim Premji is a distinguished Indian businessman. He is a graduate in Electrical Engineering from Stanford University, USA. At the age of 21, Premji joined Wipro, then his father's vegetable oil business after the sudden demise of his father. Now he is the Chairman of Wipro Corporation. A role model for young entrepreneurs across the world, Mr. Azim Premji has integrated the country's entrepreneurial tradition with professional management, based on sound values and uncompromising integrity.

Swami Chinmayananda

Swami Chinmayananda, the founder of Chinmaya Mission, was a sage and visionary. He toured tirelessly all around the world giving discourses and writing commentaries on the scriptural knowledge of Vedanta, until he left his bodily form in 1993. (See write-up at the end of this book.)

Swami Ishwarananda

Swami Ishwarananda is the dean (*ācārya*) of Chinmaya Mission Los Angeles, Bakersfield and Tustin, California. Upon completing his *brahmacārī* training in 1993 he served Chinmaya Mission Centers in Bangalore and Calcutta and eventually as resident *Ācārya* of Chinmaya Mission Los Angeles. Swamiji was given *saṁnyāsa* in February of 2000. From 2002 to 2004 he was the *ācārya* in charge of Sandeepany Sadhanalaya in Mumbai for the 12th *brahmacārī* training course. Swamiji is a dynamic speaker and has given talks on Vedanta, stress management, and management techniques. His mastery over the field of Vedanta comes through in his lucid and practical talks.

ABOUT THE AUTHORS

Swami Jyotirmayananda

Swami Jyotirmayananda was born on February 3, 1931 in Bihar, India. He embraced the ancient order of *saṁnyāsa* on February 3, 1953 at the age of 22. He served his guru, Swami Sivananda tirelessly. In March 1969 he established an ashram in Miami Florida, the Yoga Research Foundation that has become the center for international activities. Branches of this organization now exist throughout the world.

Swamini Saradapriyananda

Swamini Saradapriyananda was one of the first disciples of Swami Chinmayananda. A lawyer from Hyderabad, she gave up everything for a higher calling. She adopted orphans and elderly alike and established one of the biggest socio-economic projects from the grass roots level, now known as Chinmayaranyam. Her life was an extraordinary example of service and simplicity. She has authored several books and also translated some of Swami Chinmayananda's commentaries into Tamil. Swamini "Amma" attained *mahāsamādhi* on April 17, 2000 at Tirupati, India.

Swami Sivananda

Swami Sivananda was born on Septmber 8th, 1887 in Pattamadai in Tamil Nadu. Initially he studied medicine and migrated to Malaysia where he served as a doctor in the rubber estates. Constant contact with human suffering made him introspective and the study of philosophical literature further whetted his appetite to discover the Truth. Soon this inner urge became all-consuming and he left his post and turned homeward. Back in India, he went to Kashi and Pandharpur. After wandering for a while in Maharashtra as a mendicant, he went to Rishikesh where he met his Guru who gave him *saṁnyāsa* and the monastic name Sivananda. He now plunged into austerities of various kinds and after years of sustained self-discipline, saw the Light of God. Keen to share his new-found wisdom with seeking souls, he founded the Divine Life Society. The Master attained *mahāsamādhi* in 1963, but the Divine Life Society founded by him, the disciples he trained and the books written by him continue to carry the torch of spiritual wisdom to all corners of the globe in ever-increasing measure.

Swami Tejomayananda

Swami Tejomayananda, the spiritual head of Chinmaya Mission centers worldwide since 1993, is fulfilling the vision of his guru, Swami Chinmayananda. As Mission head, Swami Tejomayananda has already conducted more than 400 *jñāna yajña* worldwide. He has served as dean or *ācārya* of the Sandeepany Institutes of Vedanta, both in India and in California. Fluent in Hindi, Marathi and English, and lecturing and writing commentaries in all three languages he makes even the most complicated Vedantic topics clear to his audience.

Pronunciation of Sanskrit Letters

a	(but)	k	(skate)	t	⌠think or	ś	(shove)
ā	(father)	kh	(Kate)	th	⌡third	ṣ	(bushel)
i	(it)	g	(gate)	d	⌠this or	s	(so)
ī	(beet)	gh	(gawk)	dh	⌡there	h	(hum)
u	(suture)	ṅ	(sing)	n	(numb)	ṁ	(nasaliza-
ū	(pool)	c	(chunk)	p	(spin)		tion of
ṛ	(rig)	ch	(match)	ph	(loophole)		preceding
ṝ	(rrrig)	j	(John)	b	(bun)		vowel)
⌠no	jh	(jam)	bh	(rub)	ḥ	(aspira-
ḷ ⟨English	ñ	(bunch)	m	(much)		tion of
⟨equiva-	ṭ	(tell)	y	(young)		preceding
⌡lent	ṭh	(time)	r	(drama)		vowel)
e	(play)	ḍ	(duck)	l	(luck)		
ai	(high)	ḍh	(dumb)	v	(wile/vile)		
o	(toe)	n	(under)				
au	(cow)						

THE *Self-Discovery* SERIES

Meditation and Life
by Swami Chinmayananda

Self-Unfoldment
by Swami Chinmayananda

THE *Hindu Culture* SERIES

Hindu Culture: An Introduction
by Swami Tejomayananda

The Sanskrit word *Mananam* means reflection. The *Mananam Series* of books is dedicated to promoting the ageless wisdom of Vedanta, with an emphasis on the unity of all religions. Spiritual teachers from different traditions give us fresh, insightful answers to age-old questions so that we may apply them in a practical way to the dilemmas we all face in life. It is published by Chinmaya Mission West, which was founded by Swami Chinmayananda in 1975. Swami Chinmayananda pursued the spiritual path in the Himalayas, under the guidance of Swami Sivananda and Swami Tapovanam. He is credited with the awakening of India and the rest of the world to the ageless wisdom of Vedanta. He taught the logic of spirituality and emphasized that selfless work, study, and meditation are the cornerstones of spiritual practice. His legacy remains in the form of books, audio and video tapes, schools, social service projects, and Vedanta teachers who now serve their local communities all around the world.